The
RCAF
In
Alberta
A Brief History

Sic itur ad astra.
Such is the pathway to the stars.

The RCAF In Alberta
A Brief History

By
Alexandra King

1924 • RCAF Centenary • 2024

THE RCAF IN ALBERTA
A Brief History

Copyright © Alexandra King, 2024

All rights reserved. No part of this publication may be reproduced, stored in a retrieval system, or transmitted in any form or by any means, electronic, mechanical, photocopying, recording, or otherwise, without written permission of the author and publisher.

Published by Alexandra King, Edmonton, Canada

ISBN:
    Paperback   978-1-77354-557-8
        ebook   978-1-77354-558-5

Publication assistance by
PageMaster Publishing
PageMaster.ca

Foreword

Since its inception in 1924, the Royal Canadian Air Force (RCAF) has served Canadians in peace and war. The Royal Canadian Air Force Association (RCAFA) is joining many other aviation groups and organizations to celebrate the 100th Anniversary of the Royal Canadian Air Force (RCAF) and honour the service and spirit of the women and men who served in it.

Emerging from the experiences of the first world war the original Canadian Air Force was blessed with individuals like "Wop" May with imagination, determination, and the willingness to accept any challenge. The results were remarkable as wartime veterans laid the foundation of civil aviation in Canada.

The RCAF played a vital role in the Second World War, becoming the fourth-largest Allied air force with many outstanding accomplishments. One of the most significant of these was the British Commonwealth Air Training Plan (BCATP). Canada, with its geographic size and distance from the battlefield, would become the "aerodrome of democracy" where over 100,000 aircrew and countless tradesmen were trained. The BCATP had enormous social, financial, and technological impact on Canada and Canadians.

The postwar RCAF was second to none on all fronts and reached its "golden age" in the late 1950s. The RCAF made significant contributions to NATO, NORAD, and several UN operations and Peace Keeping missions.

In NATO the RCAF played a leading role in stabilizing an uncertain and threatening political situation. During the Cold War the RCAF had dozens of combat squadrons on its front lines. In the post-Cold War era, the RCAF continues to make significant contributions to protecting Canada and Canadians.

The women and men of the RCAF have always been determined, innovative, flexible, and embodied with a spirit of enthusiasm and optimism. These characteristics are the ties that bind historical facts and the stories that make up this book. These characteristics exist today in the men and women as they existed throughout the 100 years of the Royal Canadian Air Force and Canadian Air Forces that came before it.

700 (City of Edmonton) Wing Royal Canadian Air Force Association commissioned Alexandra King to write a brief history of the RCAF in Alberta to whet the appetite for military history and encourage further study. Alexandra graduated from Concordia University of Edmonton in 2021 with a Bachelor of Arts in History. She has worked in museums in various capacities for six years and started her current position as a program assistant at the Fort Heritage Precinct in late 2021. She is looking forward to becoming a curator.

T. L. "Tom" Sand
Lieutenant Colonel (Ret'd) CD
700 (City of Edmonton) Wing
Royal Canadian Air Force Association

Contents

The History of the RCAF in Alberta 1
The British Commonwealth Air Training Plan 4
    Bomber Command 17
    Albertans Overseas 24
    On the Home Front 30
Photo Gallery 33
Peacetime 47
    Mid-Canada and Pinetree Lines 51
Changes to the Air Force 58
    Nuclear Weaponry in Alberta 62
Canadians Overseas after the Second World War 68
2001 and Onwards 76
Into The Future 82
Author's Note and Acknowledgments 85
Bibliography 87

The History of the RCAF in Alberta

In 1919, following the end of the First World War, Canada stood at a crossroads. Still under the shadow of Great Britain but slowly coming into its own, the nation agreed to be a part of the International Convention for Air Navigation. This may not seem significant, but it meant that Canada was pledging military responsibility for its own air space. But how?

Air Forces were new. The idea of fighting in a plane had only just been born. Ambitious Canadian aviators found themselves having to move to Great Britain to join the Royal Air Force (RAF), which had come into its own during the Great War. A new idea would have to be created to keep Canadians at home to fulfil the requirements of the Convention. Fortunately, the Canadian government was able to acquire surplus war time equipment from Great Britain and so created the Air Board.

A far cry from an official air force, the Air Board opened its first Alberta station in the town of Morely in 1920. Located just under an hour west of Calgary on the Stoney Nakoda Reserves 142/143/144, this was one of five stations built across Canada, all of which were furnished with second hand supplies. Employment was a hard sell, since the RAF was more established and available to Canadians since Canada was still part of the British Empire, but nonetheless there were enough eager pilots about to staff the station.

The purpose of the Morely station was primarily to monitor fire conditions in the Rocky Mountains. It only operated during the summer and fall seasons, since aircraft at the time did not fly well in below zero temperatures. Winds off the Rocky Mountains meant that fabric and wood aircraft often could not take off when needed, leading to the station closing after only one year and a search beginning for a better location.

Calgary was an obvious choice. It was a business hub and had been for a long time and it was closer to the mountains than Edmonton so it would be easier to monitor fire conditions from there. There was only one problem: land around the city was very expensive. Luckily, the nearby town of High River offered an affordable option and was more than happy to host this new endeavour.

The farm land that was chosen for the base was leased for a period of two years. Construction began very quickly and consisted of a garage, an office, a workshop, 2 storage buildings, a radio tower, and wireless station for radio broadcasts. The hangers used were temporary wartime "Bessonneau" hangers that had been shipped in. These consisted of a wooden skeleton covered in tarp and had the benefit of being customizable in size as more scaffolds and additional tarps could be added fairly easily. Bessonneau hangers could be made into permanent structures simply by adding wood slats along the walls, however they remained uninsulated. Aircrafts arrived in kits on the train – some assembly required – and the first flight out of the High River Air Board Flying Operations Station took place on May 6th, 1921, just four months after construction had commenced.

The Air Board was short lived in Canada. Just two years after the High River station was completed, the Canadian Air Force replaced the Air Board and overtook operations. This did not alter the High River station's function, however, as it was still mostly used for aerial photography and monitoring fire conditions.

On April 1st, 1924, the Canadian Air Force was given the designation of Royal by King George V. And thus, High River became Alberta's very first Royal Canadian Air Force (RCAF) station.

One hundred years later and the station still stands, though it is privately owned and no longer a military establishment. Much like many RCAF stations around the province, High River wore many hats throughout its history. It played an important role in the Second World War, a role that would be recognized internationally and then quickly forgotten. The Cold War would miss High River but not the province. Alberta would house parts of the Pinetree Line, a radar warning system that was designed to intercept a nuclear attack over the Arctic Circle from Russia. And when the Cold War froze entirely, a few Albertan bases would persevere through modern military changes; contributing to Canadian efforts in NATO and United Nations missions, international peacekeeping operations, and keeping our skies full of aircrafts with the same fervour that those first Air Board pilots had 100 years ago.

The British Commonwealth Air Training Plan

CANADA AT WAR!

The headlines were clear. As of September 10th, 1939, Canada had entered the war against Nazi Germany.

This did not come as a surprise for most people. Just seven days prior, on September 3, the United Kingdom and France had both declared war in response to the German invasion of Poland. Canadians, then members of the British Empire and many with French heritage, had more than expected to join the fight. This would be a different war from the last one, however. Airborne conflict was inevitable. No longer were battlefields to be far from home, aviation technology had made it so that hundreds of kilometres could be covered in minutes. The skies of Europe could be filled with planes at any time, enemy or ally alike.

Knowing that this war would be fought in the air as much as on the ground, Britain decided that the Commonwealth should have a standardised air training plan to ensure uniformity within the air force. Navies and armies had already had hundreds of years to iron out their traditions, but the newly emerging air forces would need to condense the timeline. But where would such an endeavour take place?

The United Kingdom was not an option, as German aircraft could easily enter the airspace and shoot down pilots during training. Australia and New Zealand were too far away, not just from the United Kingdom but also the United States of America. Even if the USA was at that point staying out of the conflict, they were a large industrial nation that could easily supply parts if paid enough, so it would be a good idea to remain close to them. Suddenly Canada became the most logical option. There was plenty of open space, it was only across the Atlantic Ocean from England which was not so far away that transporting recruits there was impossible to but was too far for German planes to make regular raids, and it was America's closest neighbour.

After a little hesitation from Prime Minister William Lyon Mackenzie King, who worried that this would be a step backwards into British control over the nation, it was eventually decided that Canada would host the British Commonwealth Air Training Plan (BCATP). Even Prime Minister King would eventually concede that the signing of this agreement in 1939 was an incredibly significant decision by the Canadian government.

Construction was swift. Many bases were built on farmland, so the harvest had to come off the fields before buildings could be put up. This would happen in early fall and the bases were generally operational before the New Year, with the first flights taking place shortly thereafter. At the peak of the program there were 94 schools across the country, nine of which were located in Alberta.

All recruits would begin at Manning Depot where they would undergo basic training which included physical and mental exercise as well as learning to meet military standards of cleanliness. They would then go to an Initial Training School (ITS) where they would not only learn the basics of flying such as mathematics, navigation, and aerodynamics, but they would also be split into two streams based on their individual skills.

It would be untrue to say that some students were not good enough to become pilots or that they failed to meet the qualifications to be pilots. More accurately, some students were better at jobs like navigation and wireless radio operation. Schools for both roles as well as bomber/gunnery schools and maintenance stations were also peppered across the province. Those who did have the right skills to be pilots, on the other hand, would move onto Elementary Flying Training Schools (EFTS) where they would undergo eight weeks of training to become competent in flying a plane. There were six such schools located in Alberta during the war.

Though High River's airfield had been closed for a decade, it was reopened as No 5 EFTS in 1941. This was done because the previous location of No 5 EFTS in Lethbridge, had too many delayed flights due to high winds. At one point the senior class was 17 days behind schedule with only 14 days left in the course. High River, having been a successful airfield before the war, was chosen as a suitable replacement. The Calgary Flying Club had been using the base for recreational purposes in the intervening decade, so some facilities still existed. However, this was going to be a much bigger operation than before. So construction began on a large permanent hangar (this time insulated so that training could continue in the winter), a guard house, a gymnasium, barracks, a storehouse, a mess hall, and classroom facilities. The mess hall was furnished with dinnerware that was all made in province at the Medalta pottery plant in Medicine Hat, stamped with a blue RCAF crest.

In June of 1941, which was the proposed move-in date for the school, the site was still mostly mud. Only two barracks had running water and the kitchen lacked both water and gas hook ups. Some contractors were so close to quitting that they had to be bribed with beer to stay on the job. Despite this, the school opened in September of 1941 with a crowd of 2500 people in attendance as troops marched in formation and a flying demonstration swooped overhead.

In the town of High River there was a construction boom as well, as the hope was that the existence of the base would bring an influx of new people, both military and civilian into town. Land by the river was divided into lots in the hopes of prompting new residential construction and the town council managed to get the provincial government to pay to have their main street paved. There was a small population boom as more personnel moved to the base. Though recruits were generally younger, some instructors and civilian personnel brought with them wives and children. Many homes in High River offered up spare bedrooms or make-shift suites to rent to families who were following their husbands to the base.

There was also a noticeable uptick in business at many stores in town–including the drug store, hotel beer parlour, and the movie theatre–as new families settled in, and both staff and students alike ventured off base for evening fun. The High River Creamery landed the supply contract for EFTS No 5, which meant that many local farmers increased the size of their dairy herds in order to keep up with demand.

This economic boom was a common theme around BCATP schools, especially in rural areas of the province. The town of Nanton, for example, never hosted a school of their own but the mayor frequented functions at the No 2 Flight Instructor School in the nearby town of Vulcan and many staff lived in Nanton and were bussed to the base.

Entertainment and socialisation were considered a vital service that could be provided by the town. Most of the men at the school were young and used to going out with friends or being around family. Being so far away from home and undergoing intensive training that often left very little downtime meant that there was a fear that homesickness and depression could set in, lowering troop morale. As a result, townspeople were urged to join in on base festivities and students were given opportunities to join in on town fun. In High River, it was decided that an event should be held every two or three weeks with several town committees sharing the duties of planning with the school. Dances were held on base so that personnel could make a reasonable curfew (lessons did not stop for fun!) and the base theatre welcomed townspeople to the films being shown three times a week, many of which were early releases, meaning High River was seeing movies before anywhere else in the province. The local newspaper also urged families to phone the base and offer to host students for dinner at their home–all they had to do was tell the base how many of the young men they could accommodate, and the base would send the students out for a home cooked meal. Though there are no exact numbers for how many families took this offer, the town was very eager to help with morale. Many of the women had said goodbye to husbands, brothers, and sons who had joined up, and so felt that if they could not have their own family around, they would offer their support to someone else's instead.

Socialising was not just limited to the closest town, however. Many schools also had their own orchestras and minstrel shows, who would perform at their home school and tour to other nearby schools.

As well as student morale, there was a more practical need to provide social events that included both the civilians from town and the airmen from base: most of the staff at a BCATP base were not military personnel at all. Service and maintenance to the aircrafts, office and accounting work, food services, medical and dental care, security, and even most of the flying instruction was carried out by civilians, generally hired from the surrounding communities.

In fact there were very few military personnel on base who were not students. Only the Chief Flying Instructors and the Commanding Officers could be guaranteed to be military members.

So creating social events would also act like staff bonding, so that the civilians employed by the schools and the military members attending the schools would blend together as a cohesive team.

Many civilian instructors had tried to join up but were either reassigned or already so good at flying that it made more sense to have them teach than fight. In the latter case, there is no better example than Wop May.

―――

Born Wilfried Ried May on March 20, 1896, "Wop" got his start in aviation during the First World War. He earned the title of flying ace when, in April 1918, he was involved in the dogfight that resulted in Manfred von Richthofen, who was better known as the Red Baron, being shot down. Wop had drawn the attention of the German flying ace and begun to lead him in a chase when Arthur Roy Brown, another Canadian pilot, fired the shot that downed the infamous aircraft. (There is some debate as to whether Arthur Roy Brown officially killed the Red Baron, as Australian machine gunners on the ground during the dogfight also fired on the plane at the same time.)

After the war, May worked as a barnstormer, meaning he performed aerial tricks for exhibitions and rodeos. He also leant his services to the first ever aerial police chase, where he flew police Constable William Nixon from Edmonton to Edson to capture John Larson, a murder suspect. A few years later he was hired by the RCMP to help search for The Mad Trapper of Rat River, who was wanted for murder under the name Albert Johnson. May was the one who saw Johnson and reported the suspect's location to RCMP. He also retrieved Johnson's body after he was killed in a gunfight with law enforcement.

When war broke out, May joined up and, instead of being sent back to combat, was assigned to No 2 Air Observer School (AOS) in Edmonton, where he taught students how to use navigational tools to keep aeroplanes on track when they were on missions. This was more challenging than just using a map, as most missions were intended to be flown at night and cities across Europe had implemented blackout restrictions, making it nearly impossible to simply look down from the aircraft and see where in Europe you were flying. Towards the end of the war, the Allies would begin using radar (to conceal this invention from the Germans, the British government ran a campaign that eating carrots had improved the vision of their pilots) but at first navigators had to learn how to plot their course with very little instrumental assistance. May would have used a number of these navigation techniques during the First World War as well as during his time between the wars when he was hired by the police.

Because of his flying skills and the number of student pilots under his command, May was often called upon in search and rescue missions during the war. Though the Alaska Highway began construction in 1942, it was still easier for us troops to fly between Alaska and the "Lower 48" states than contend with a partially finished road, especially when it came to moving troops up north. This placed Edmonton in a flight corridor between the two. Because of its remote location and close proximity to Russia–which was an Allied nation during the Second World War–there were serious concerns that Japanese forces would invade the United States and Canada via Alaska. A defence front was placed up north and the US flew troops up via Edmonton. Unfortunately, flight conditions were often dangerous. To help with the large number of rescues, May proposed a civilian run para-rescue squad.

Officially established in 1943 this specially trained rescue team would parachute in to help potential survivors of a crash, evacuating those who needed medical attention and assessing whether the aircraft could be salvaged. This rescue model was eventually adopted by the RCAF and is still used in search and rescue operations today.

For his services to the American army through these rescue missions, Wop May was awarded the American Medal of Freedom in 1947. In his home country, he was inducted in Canada's Aviation Hall of Fame in 1974, an award which recognized both his military and non-military aviation pursuits.

Wop May was not the only Canadian Aviation Hall of Famer who worked with the BCATP. Dennis K. Yorath, who was the managing director of EFTS No 5 High River, was inducted into the Hall of Fame in 1973 as a direct result of his work during the war. Yorath had become a pilot in High River in 1928 and was the son of the Calgary Aero Club's first president, so during wartime he was an easy fit to run a large-scale aviation operation.

Once recruits had completed their eight-week course at an EFTS, they were transferred to a Service Flying Training School (SFTS) where they would acquire more advanced flying skills that would become useful when engaging the enemy overseas, generally separating students by those who were skilled enough to be fighter pilots and those more suited to less technical flying tasks. Out in Fort Macleod, No 7 SFTS is a great example of the quick turnaround expected by the training plan, as the first graduating class of pilots were presented their wings in March of 1941, just three months after the school had opened.

Generally, recruits were transferred to a different town for each level, as most towns only had one or two schools nearby, however Calgary was a hub for the training plan. It hosted two Service Flying Training Schools (No 3 and No 37) and No 2 Wireless School, which taught students how to operate radios. However, it was also home to No 10 Repair Depot and No 11 Equipment Depot, which meant planes were often flown there for larger maintenance projects that could not be completed at individual flying schools. The reason for this high concentration of BCATP facilities was that Calgary hosted No 4

Training Command Headquarters, meaning it was the head of the BCATP for Western Canada, overseeing bases across British Columbia, Alberta, and most of Saskatchewan between October 1941 and November 1944.

In June of 1941, No 10 Repair Depot was moved to Calgary from Regina, Saskatchewan, which had also been the location of No 4 Training Command Headquarters from April 1940 until the move.

Though many schools moved locations as needed, not every school remained open for the duration of the war. No 2 Flight Instructor School (FIS), previously based in Claresholm, had broken ground in Vulcan, Alberta in September of 1941. This school remained under construction for ten months, which was much longer than usual. 52 buildings, including 7 hangers, were built along with paved runways, powerlines, sewage, heat and water systems.

Vulcan had been an airfield since the 1930s, when a landing area was built for planes carrying mail between Calgary and Lethbridge. The "beacon," as it was called, created a small housing boom as many employees brought their wives and children with them when they moved there. These existing facilities were likely the reason Vulcan became one of only three Flight Instructor Schools in Canada, and the only one operating outside of Ontario. It was a very successful school with an estimated 750 students graduating from it in the two years it was open. At the peak of the base, there were 1300 personnel and 163 aircrafts. However, it was moved to Pearce, Alberta in 1943 and closed shortly after. The Pearce location quickly filled with No 19 SFTS. This did not slow anything down, however, No 19 SFTS still saw 860 graduates get their wings (the term for officially becoming a licenced military pilot) there between 1943 and 1945.

Generally, like other towns, the relationship between the base and civilians was good, although in the fall of 1942 a disgruntled farmwife brandished a shotgun at a few airmen who were trying to disassemble a plane that had gotten caught in a barbed wire fence a few miles from the station. Luckily no one was injured but the fence was repaired at gunpoint. These kinds of small spats did tend to happen. In Pearce, there was a brief complaint that recruits were flying so low they once dented the top of a car. There were dedicated low flying zones that students were required to be familiar with prior to solo flights, however it is not clear whether these were implemented before or after incidents like this.

Not all such crashes ended with funny tales to tell. In 1942, for example, a plane from Claresholm and a plane from High River collided midair. Though the occupants of the plane from Claresholm were able to make an emergency landing, the instructor and student in the plane from High River were killed in the crash. Canada-wide, 856 trainees were killed in accidents during the training program. However, by 1944 there was only an average of one death for every 22,388 hours that students spent in the air. Though that still sounds like too many for most, this was incredibly small numbers compared to those killed on actual missions overseas.

Recruits not only came from across Canada, but the training plan also serviced air forces from across the Commonwealth. This meant that recruits from as far away as Australia and New

Zealand might be seen roaming the streets of small Alberta towns. No 31 EFTS in DeWinton noted that many of its students were escapees of Nazi Germany who had joined up with the intention to free their homelands themselves. There were also a great deal of Americans in the BCATP who had crossed the border to sign up despite their home country officially staying neutral at first. Their numbers dropped noticeably after the attack on Pearl Harbour in 1941, as the United States Army Air Force (USAAF) began recruiting and many current students left to join up in their home country instead.

Nor were recruits all male. By 1941, the RCAF had established the Women's Division (WD) and was recruiting women in the thousands. Intended to fill non-combatant roles that were being left empty as men deployed overseas, members of the WD served on base as radio operators, nurses, drivers, clerical staff, and radar operators. Eventually they began to fill even more roles such as packing parachutes and overseeing maintenance on aeroplanes, their instruments, and the meteorological equipment used on base. Packing parachutes was not a one-time job either, as each chute had to be inspected once every thirty days, which meant unpacking it, and any minor repairs needed were made on base, likely by a member of the WD.

Many women were in the air with their male counterparts as part of the Air Transport Auxiliary (ATA). The ATA ferried aircraft between different locations, flying them from factory to training field, and from training field to repair depot when needed. This freed up male pilots to continue teaching and learning at the schools and left the women free to soar over the prairies. Many women would have been employed at No 10 Repair Depot in Calgary, which oversaw major repairs on aircrafts from all the schools overseen by No 4 Training Command Headquarters. ATA pilots would fly planes into the depot (which was located at what is now the junction of Crowchild Trail and Glenmore Trail) from bases across BC, Alberta, and Saskatchewan and then use the No 3 SFTS runway (also located in Calgary) for test flights before flying them back to their home bases.

Outside of Alberta, the ATA also saw women taking aircraft across the Atlantic Ocean to be used in Europe. 309,011 transatlantic flights were made during the war, covering large expanses of ocean that even some pilots today find a terrifying task. There was nothing between these women and drowning except for a few hundred feet and the hard to distinguish horizon. This job has interestingly not remained a woman's work in modern day, as there are presently no immersion suits designed by the Canadian Military for overseas flights available in women's sizes.

By the end of the war, there were over 17,000 women in service in the Women's Division alone, meaning that women made up 23% of the entire RCAF. Of these 17,000 women, 1500 would serve overseas during the war.

One such woman was Frieda Smith of Strome, Alberta. While working as a bank clerk in Edmonton she enlisted as a pay accounts clerk with the RCAF Women's Division. She trained in Toronto and was posted to the RCAF Station in Rockcliffe, near Ottawa. She became a Section Officer (S/O) in 1943 and posted to No 3 SFTS in Calgary before she was sent to Yorkshire, England in 1944, where she remained working for the RCAF until 1946 when she was demobilised. She returned to her work as a bank clerk after the war, this time in Calgary where she passed away in 2006. For her wartime service,

S/O Smith was awarded the Defence Medal, the Canadian Volunteer Service Medal, and the 1939-1945 War Medal.

As far as men went, a total of 131,553 students (all of whom would have been male) graduated from the BCATP. Of this, 72,835 became part of the RCAF, ready to serve Canada overseas in the war.

Bomber Command

The BCTAP was not designed to train up a bunch of pilots to stay at home in Canada. Their end goal was to have an effective and uniformly trained air force to work under what was known as the "Bomber Command."

Bomber Command refers to the command centre that oversaw a 2000-day operation in which Allied planes carried out missions across Nazi-occupied airspaces. Generally, as the name suggests, the goal was to drop bombs on specific targets–primarily factories or industrially significant sites but often on civilian homes as well. This also came with the expectation of the enemy returning fire, so there were often multiple aircraft on a bombing raid with different tasks. Some might, for example, be charged with engaging enemy planes in dog fights while others were to fly low and shoot at anti-aircraft artillery to keep the aircraft loaded with bombs from being shot down.

Raids tended to take place at night, as aircraft could fly without lights, sneaking in and out of enemy territory with only the whine of an engine to betray their presence. The trip was a long one, especially when Bomber Command ordered pilots to target the city of Berlin. The Luftwaffe (Nazi Germany's air force) had begun a bombing campaign on London, hitting civilian infrastructure as well as industrial targets, which prompted Allied forces to respond in kind. Sometimes planes were too damaged from enemy fire or too low on fuel to make it all the way from England to Berlin and back again. Many pilots and their crews had to "ditch" their plane over the ocean or, even worse, in enemy territory.

Each aircraft was crewed by at least one pilot and a navigator, however larger bombers would also have flight engineer, a wireless radio operator, two air gunners, and a bomb aimer (also called a bombardier) who could also man the guns at the nose of the aircraft if needed. These seven men were often very close, as they literally placed their lives in each other's hands every time they went out on a raid. It is estimated that for every 100 men in Bomber Command, 45 would be killed, 6 seriously injured, and 8 captured as Prisoners of War. Except for the Nazi U-boat force, Bomber Command suffered the highest losses of any force during the war.

Hazel Taylor knew this truth all too well when she received a Memorial Cross during the war. The Memorial Cross, more commonly known as the Silver Cross, is a medal given to the widows and mothers of service members killed in combat. Mrs. Taylor was awarded the Memorial Cross after the death of her husband, F/O Fredrick S. Taylor.

Taylor had grown up in Fort Saskatchewan, Alberta and he and his wife had been married in Edmonton 1941, however he was working at the Essondale Mental Hospital (now Riverview Hospital) in British Columbia when he signed up and had been since 1939. The couple lived in British Columbia and had one child; a son named David. F/O Taylor trained at EFTS No 5 in High River before receiving his wings in Dauphin, Manitoba. He arrived in Britain in 1942 and records indicate that he was an average student who showed considerable promise with time and practice. However, in 1943 the engine of his aircraft failed during a night flight and he crashed landed in Yorkshire, England. According to his records the flight was "non-operational," meaning he was training at the time.

His wife, Hazel, and his mother, Lily (or Lilly, records vary), both received a Memorial Cross, which would be engraved with F/O Taylor's name and service number. Both Hazel and Lily would have been allowed to wear the cross at any time. And though the cross was something worn proudly by its recipients, it was—and still is—the worst award one could receive, as it came without the man who had won it.

One of the first raids that many Canadians participated in was Operation Millennium, a mass bombing of Cologne, Germany on the night of May 30/31, 1942. One of the men on this raid was Flying Officer Stanley Gordon King (he went by Gord as his father was also Stanley) from Winnipeg. King had joined up in September of 1940 and was originally told that there were too many pilots. His second-choice job was a gunner but he was ultimately selected to run the wireless radio on board the plane, meaning he was the only source of communication, outside of each other, that a flight crew would have when they were on their life threatening mission. While in training he made friends with a doctor who eventually helped him to get into flight school. Flying Officer King finished the last bit of his training overseas and was on his first leave (also called rest tour) when the raid was set to take place.

The RAF, RCAF, and Royal Australian Air Force (RAAF) were all contributing as much as possible to the raid, but resources were stretched rather thin. Training aircrafts were being used in addition to the actual bombers so some crew had not finished their training when they were told they were going to be on the operation. Many, like Flying Officer King, were called off their rest tours and told to report back to take part in the raid.

The operation was so large that each aircraft was assigned a height at which to fly as well as a time at which to take off, as there was very real fear that the aircrafts would collide midair. Communication in the air was not reliable as not all of the aircrafts were equipped with "Gee" radios, which offered a level of secrecy not seen in traditional wireless radio which could be overheard by enemy operators. There were also only 90 minutes assigned to the operation–compared to typical 100 bomber raids which were given a time frame of four hours. The small window was in the hopes that the sheer number of aircraft would overwhelm German defences. And it did. Higher losses were recorded in the first wave of bombers than others, meaning the defences had been unable to keep up with the later waves. In the city of Cologne, it was recorded that 2500 fires were started, and 13,000 buildings were destroyed. Only about 2500 of the buildings hit were commercial or industrial, the rest were residential.

Despite massive residential destruction, there was not a very high civilian death toll. Only 500 citizens of Cologne were reported killed the night of the raid, with about 5000 injured, which was not considered a high number for a wartime air raid. There were an estimated 45,000 citizens bombed out of their houses, however, and it was estimated that between 130,000 and 150,000 of the 700,000 citizens of Cologne fled the city afterwards.

When the raid was first planned, Prime Minister Sir Winston Churchill estimated that 100 aircrafts would likely be lost. However, the final number given by the RAF (who was overseeing the Bomber Command) was only 41. Of these 41, only two were lost in a midair collision. The rest were shot down by German defences.

In the wake of this success, a second 1000 bomber raid was called, this time targeting the city of Bremen. It was on this raid that Flying Officer King's plane was hit.

For men who were forced to bail out of their planes there were two likely outcomes: evade capture or become a Prisoner of War (POW). Crew members would be trained on how to handle these situations prior to being sent out on missions. There were "escape kits" for each crew member which would often include maps to help them avoid being captured. Europe was also filled with a number of organized anti-Nazi resistances as well as other civilians who were willing to help Allied airmen. It was these networks who would provide shelter, medical care, a change of clothing, and even forged documents to help airmen pass safely through occupied territory. For those who were not able to evade capture, such as Flying Officer King, they would become POWs until war's end. Though King did successfully bail out of his plane, his parachute got tangled in a tree and when trying to get untangled he fell to the ground and knocked himself unconscious. When he awoke, he was turned in to German authorities by farmers that found him and he was taken to one of the most well-known POW camps, Stalag Luft III, which was also where another Albertan, Flight Lieutenant (F/L) Henry J. Birkland was prisoner.

F/L Birkland was raised in Calgary, Alberta but was working in British Columbia when war broke out. His father had immigrated from Norway and his mother from the Holstein region of Denmark (which is now a part of Germany). Birkland, who went by Hank, joined the RCAF in Vancouver in 1940. His plane was shot down in November of 1941 and he was sent to Stalag Luft III, which was 160 kilometres southeast of Berlin outside of the town of Żagań, Poland.

Stalag Luft III was considered a model POW camp, having been deemed so during an inspection by the International Red Cross. The camp was also specifically for officers, which generally meant that better living conditions were available as officers were seen as higher status than enlisted men and therefore afforded more privileges. Despite this, food rations were meagre, and men relied heavily on packages delivered by the Red Cross. According to Flying Officer King, the guards at Stalag Luft III did not interact with the prisoners much outside of two or three regular roll calls each day. Prisoners organised sport teams and taught each other classes based on what they had done for jobs/education before the war.

The location of the camp had originally been chosen because it was deemed too difficult to escape, however, in January of 1943, prisoners in the camp, including F/L Birkland and Flying Officer King devised a plan to dig three tunnels out of the camp, a plan that would later become known as the Great Escape.

Codenamed "Tom", "Dick", and "Harry", the tunnels were concealed carefully within barracks or, in the case of "Dick", the shower, and slowly dug out with metal buckets, hammers, and crowbars. Bed boards were used to reinforce the tunnel, which was only 2 feet square for most of its length, and there was a rail track system that would transport the tunnelers– and hopefully the escapees–to the end of the line. All those working on the actual tunnelling part of the operation were Canadian personnel, most of whom had experience with mining. F/L Birkland, for example, had been employed by a mining company in British Columbia before he enlisted, where he had done hard rock mining, making him more than suitable to help plan and execute an escape tunnel under the camp.

On the night of March 24th, 1944, the breakout began. Approximately 200 prisoners were ready and waiting, many with civilian clothes, German military uniforms, and even forged documents (created by artistically inclined POWs) to facilitate their escape. Flying Officer King had been designated as escapee number 141. In the meantime, he operated the pump that sent air into the tunnel, ensuring that no one suffocated on their way out. Unfortunately, the tunnel had come up just a few feet short of the trees and the 77th prisoner through the tunnel was spotted by guards. F/L Birkland had been one of the 76 to make it out before they were sighted. Of these 76 escapees, only 3 would make it back to safety.

The escape was considered such an embarrassment to Nazi Germany that Adolf Hitler himself ordered a nationwide search for the escapees. Birkland was caught, along with 50 other men, and, instead of being returned to the camp, was executed enroute. By May of 1944 his father had been informed that his son was presumed to have been killed in the escape, something that was confirmed in June of the same year when Birkland's death certificate was officially signed.

Birkland, along with the other soldiers who were recaptured and executed, was cremated at Stalag Luft III by German Gestapo members, many of whom were later tried in a military court for their role in the executions. (The manner in which the executions had been carried out was against the Geneva

Conventions, as the prisoners had been successfully recaptured and therefore should not have been killed.)

At some point a memorial had been constructed but in 1948 it was found to have been damaged, so the men's ashes were moved to Poznan Old Garrison Cemetery in Poland, where they would be cared for by the Imperial War Graves Commission.

Albertans Overseas

Though there were many training schools across Alberta, recruits could be sent anywhere in the country to study and when they were sent overseas it was similarly widespread. Units were organised by country of origin—meaning that Australians, Brits, and New Zealanders would not be in the same squadrons despite all having trained in Canada. Canadian units were all assigned numbers between 400 and 450 as an easy way to identify them. Sometimes there were members of a squadron not from the same country as the squadron was assigned to, but that was relatively rare and generally indicated that the person had joined the RCAF in Canada despite being from a different country. This might happen, for example, if someone had recently moved to Canada or perhaps had wanted to join but found that their own country had not joined the fighting, which was the case for many Americans who sought to sign up before the attack on Pearl Harbour.

Unlike Army Regiments, where you signed up for the RCAF did not affect what Squadron you would be assigned to. However, many squadrons were "adopted" by cities back home and proudly identified themselves as having been so, like 418 Squadron which proudly began calling itself the "City of

Edmonton" Squadron after the city took it upon itself to pay special attention to the members.

418 operated as train busters, meaning they would fly low over Nazi-occupied territory, bombing trains that were known to be carrying supplies. They also swooped low over German airfields, opening fire upon the infrastructure and its occupants, which was particularly dangerous as they had to get within the range of the machine guns stationed at each airfield. They participated in the 1942 Dieppe Raid (also called Operation Jubilee), where they provided air support as ground troops attempted but ultimately failed to liberate the coastal town of Dieppe, France from Nazi occupation, meaning 418 had to provide air support for a quick evacuation as well.

Except for a tail gunner from Mexico, squadron members were British subjects (Canada did not have its own citizenship until two years after the war ended), many of them from Northern Alberta. Because of this connection, Pilot Officer (P/O) Gordy Williamson wrote home to suggest the city of Edmonton adopt the squadron. The commanding officer of No 4 Training Command Headquarters in Calgary said there was no real history of this, suggesting instead that the city send care packages of cigarettes and other small comforts. Ignoring Calgary's suggestion, Edmonton officially adopted the squadron in March of 1944. The Hudson's Bay Company store in the city packaged up cigarettes to sell to troops and there were subscription-based care packages that one could pay to send to the soldiers. These comforts were a welcome morale booster as by this time 418 had shifted its focus to V1 defence.

V1 bombs were unmanned explosives that flew between 300 and 3,000 feet in altitude, reaching speeds of up to 370 miles per hour (595 km/hr). They were incredibly deadly when they were launched on London in the later years of the war, and it was members of 418 Squadron that perfected a rather daring method of taking them out.

Russ Bannock and Don MacFayden came up with a system of following the bomb until it was under the nose of the plane. Once the bomb had just disappeared from sight, they would spin the plane into a dive, lining the plane up and opening fire on the bomb, causing it to explode. At that point they had usually lost visual, being surrounded by smoke and fire, and would have to pull up and fly away as fast as possible to avoid damage to the plane or any further risk to themselves.

When the V2 rocket debuted shortly after it was found to be impossible to intercept them in the air, so instead 418 Squadron would go on missions referred to as "Big Ben" to find their launch sites. Much like before, these were often low flying forays into enemy territory within range of machine gun nests.

418 Squadron was disbanded in September of 1945 in Volkel, Netherlands. However, just a few months later in April 1946, 418 Squadron was reformed in its adoptive city of Edmonton. This makes the squadron rather unique in that it was adopted by an Albertan city and then worked in Alberta after the war. Many other units either disbanded permanently or were reformed in places that were not the ones that had adopted them in wartime. For example, the other current active air force squadrons in Alberta (as of 2023) were not identified as "Albertan" squadrons when they were formed during the war but nonetheless came to find their home here.

408 "Goose" Squadron, currently based at Canadian Forces Base (CFB) Edmonton, was formed in Yorkshire, England in 1942 and originally adopted by Kingsville, Ontario. After

being disbanded in Nova Scotia, the squadron was reformed in Rockville, Ontario in 1949.

409, 410, 417 and 419 Squadrons all currently operate out of CFB Cold Lake. The 409 "Nighthawks" were formed in England in 1941, adopted by the city of Victoria, British Columbia, and disbanded in the Netherlands in 1945, being reformed in Comox, BC. The 410 "Cougars" were formed in Scotland in 1941, adopted by the city of St. John, New Brunswick, and disbanded in the Netherlands in June of 1945 before being reformed in St. Hubert, Quebec in 1948. The 417 "City of Windsor" squadron was formed in England in 1941 and was the only Canadian squadron in the Desert Air Force, doing most of their combat flying over North Africa and the Middle East. After North Africa was liberated from Nazi Occupation, the squadron was sent to Italy where they supported the British Army during the Sicilian and Italian campaigns, being disbanded in Treviso, Italy in June of 1945. They were reformed in Rivers, Manitoba in 1947. Finally, the 419 "Moose" were formed in England in 1941, adopted by the city of Kamloops, BC, and disbanded in Nova Scotia in 1945 only to be reformed in North Bay, Ontario in 1954.

The only other squadron currently operational in Alberta is the 401 "Rams," who actually predate all the previous squadrons and, indeed, the RCAF itself. It was formed in the First World War as No 1 Squadron in response to the complaints that Canadians had to join the British RAF since Canada did not have its own air force. Despite the Treaty of Versailles calling for air control, 401 was disbanded in 1920, since the Air Board was better suited to peacetime. 401 was reformed and disbanded several times during the interwar period under various names but was officially renumbered to 401 in 1941 while stationed in Yorkshire, England. They were adopted by the city of Westmount, Quebec (an affluent English-speaking enclave of Montreal). The 401 "Rams" also participated in the Dieppe Raid and were made into a reserve unit after the war, having been reformed in Montreal. They currently serve out of CFB Cold Lake.

The reason for so many squadrons being disbanded in the Netherlands was the fact that the Canadian army had liberated much of the country by April of 1945. It was decided by Allied forces that liberating armies would remain in newly freed areas to help with recovery efforts such as repairing roads and buildings, supply chain management, medical aid, and reinstallation of the country's government. However, not as many military units were needed in post-war efforts as had been for fighting. So, units were slowly disbanded as the need for them grew less and less. This mirrored what was happening at home in Canada. BCATP schools had been slowly closing since 1944 when, after the successful landing in Normandy, France on D-Day, the war turned in favour of the Allies and there was less need to train new air crew. This did not mean there was less need for air crew, but simply that the war might now be over before many of the new recruits ever saw combat, so the schools did not need to be churning out thousands of qualified pilots, gunners, wireless operators, and navigators as they had in earlier years.

By April of 1945, only the region of Holland in the Netherlands was still under Nazi occupation. North and South Holland are coastal counties within the country, and with

Allied forces occupying the land around them and having dominance over the sea, surrender by occupying forces felt inevitable. However, it did not come as quickly as many had hoped. The Dutch people had suffered greatly towards the end of the war, with the food supply chain of occupying Nazi forces completely disrupted by Allied attack. At that point in the war, frozen potatoes, tulip bulbs, and even family pets had become the only source of food for many.

Having seen how critical the situation was when they liberated other parts of the country, the RCAF decided to fly ahead of any formal surrenders, dropping not bombs but parcels of food. This was Operation Manna, and it was considered by some the most important mission they would fly for the whole of the war.

Nazi machine guns held their fire as a total of 3298 bombers were flown over the country over the course of nine days, each laden with 4000 pounds of food that would float to the ground with little parachutes attached. This was followed by another 2200 American planes (who called their efforts Operation Chowhound) and then 200 Allied army trucks in Operation Faust, which involved driving straight behind German lines even though they could still be shot at. Eventually over 11,000 tons of food were delivered in the days leading up the surrender.

In Italy, the 417 "City of Windsor" Squadron was flying above the skies in the longest campaign that Canadians would engage in during the war.

The Sicilian and Italian campaigns (usually collectively referred to as the Italian campaign) lasted from July of 1943 until February of 1945. Prior to being in the Italian Campaign, 417 had flown in the North African campaign, providing air support over the Suez Canal in Egypt. North Africa was liberated from Nazi occupation in 1942 and so 417 was reassigned and by 1943 they were in Sicily supporting ground troops as they spent nearly one month slowly inching their way to meet up with British and American counterparts.

By the fall of 1943, the assault on Italy began, starting at the tip of the "boot" and working upwards. 417 was just behind the liberating forces, who declared Rome to have officially fallen on June 4th, 1944–just 48 hours before the D-Day Invasions began on the north coast of France. 417 troops continued north, fighting their last aerial battle over Treviso in 1945. In total they flew 12,116 flights and lost 28 aircrew (7 were killed, 11 presumed dead, 8 captured as POWs, and 2 managed to become evaders). Once Italy was liberated, 417 was disbanded, like many other Canadian squadrons who were not needed for peacetime reconstruction.

On the Home Front

The RCAF did not send all its aircrew overseas during the war. Many were scattered across the country with the RCAF Home War Establishment. Units performed a variety of duties including transporting aircrafts, paratrooper training, instrument calibration, overseas airmail, and aerial photography.

Support was also needed on the coasts to provide protection against naval attacks and there were very real fears of an attack from either Germany or Japan. In fact, between 1944 and 1945, Japan launched paper balloons filled with hydrogen and loaded with explosives over North America. 9,000 balloons were launched total, 20 of which were shot down by RCAF pilots over Alberta. Because the balloons were mostly launched in winter and spring, however, they did not cause major damage within the province.

Edmonton was also becoming a major hub of travel as the USAAF built a base just north of the city in 1943. The Namao base was part of what was called the NorthWest Staging Route: a series of airports that connected Great Falls, Montana with Fairbanks, Alaska. Edmonton was a critical stop along this route, as it was one of the last major settlements before aircraft had to fly over long stretches of wilderness.

This was very similar to the days of the Yukon and Alaska gold rushes, when miners would travel overland through the North-West Territories into the gold fields if they wanted to avoid the Chilkoot Pass. Edmonton, at the time, was the last major settlement until Dawson City, Yukon, meaning that prospectors would have one last chance to repair or purchase necessary gear and supplies before spending months in the bush. They could, of course, trade for food and clothing with the First Nations peoples and Inuit who lived in the north, but gold mining supplies such as shovels and other metal tools were something they had to bring themselves.

It made sense, then, that Edmonton would serve a similar function for air travel. Before the completion of the Alaska Highway in 1942, American planes on their way north would stop at Blatchford field in Edmonton. However, being the city airport and a BCATP school and a stopping point to the northernmost American state, the area was soon a little crowded. So Namao was chosen as an alternative.

Canada technically did pay for the work to be done when building the Namao base, hoping that Canadians would be able to fill the jobs, but most of the construction ended up being done by the US Army Corps of Engineers. By December of 1944 the Namao airport was world renowned, and it was suggested, after the war, that it be used as an international airport for the city of Edmonton. However, it was ultimately handed over to the 418 "City of Edmonton" Squadron.

Photo Gallery

WILFRID "WOP" MAY (C. 1920)
A GREAT WAR FLYING ACE, MAY MANAGED AIR OBSERVER SCHOOL NO. 2 IN EDMONTON AND HELPED CREATE THE SEARCH AND RESCUE MODEL THAT IS STILL USED BY THE RCAF TODAY

F/L Henry J. Birkland of Calgary, Alberta, one of the many Canadians who dug Tunnel "Harry" for the Great Escape from Stalag Luft III POW camp.

He was executed by German prison guards in 1944.

Photo credit: veterans.gc.ca

HEADQUARTERS FOR MADE-TO-MEASURE
R.C.A.F. and R.A.F. UNIFORMS
Fit Guaranteed
HAND TAILORED FROM IMPORTED FABRICS
SUITS AND COATS TAILORED TO MEASURE.

Clothes from well-known firms . . . .
HOUSE OF STONE - TIP TOP
W. R. JOHNSTON

DRY CLEANING - REPAIRING - PRESSING

J. H. GOLIGHTLY
Merchant Tailor

HIGH RIVER - - - - - **ALBERTA**

An advertisement in the local paper at High River showing how local businesses were very involved in military life.

Photo courtesy of the Museum of the Highwood

Dennis K. Yorath, manager of No 5 EFTS and Aviation Hall of Fame inductee, pictured at his desk at No 5 in High River during the war

Photo courtesy of Museum of the Highwood

TIGER MOTH AIRPLANES LINED UP AT NO 5 EFTS HIGH RIVER

Photo courtesy of the Museum of the Highwood

A SAMPLE OF THE DISHES USED AT BRITISH COMMONWEALTH AIR TRAINING PLAN SCHOOLS, ALL MADE WITHIN ALBERTA AND STAMPED WITH THE RCAF LOGO.

Photo courtesy of Medelta in the Historic Clay District

The Wireless Operations training classroom at No 5 EFTS High River. Operators could continue their training at No 2 Wireless School in Calgary, which was the only dedicated Wireless School in the province.

Photo courtesy of the Museum of the Highwood

A "Passing Out Parade" or graduation from No 5 EFTS High River (undated)

Photo courtesy of the Museum of the Highwood

R.C.A.F. Pilots Log Book Endorsations

Signatures and date in the appropriate places indicate that the person signing certifies that the appropriate requirements have been fulfilled

When	Circumstances	Date	Certification by Signature
Before solo flying	I have read and understood station Flying Orders, the file of information for Pilots and notices for Pilots	8 FEB 1944	F. Lawrence Student
Before Flying Solo	I have been instructed in and fully understand the operation of the hydraulic gear, gasoline and brake system; and I am familiar with the cockpit drill, emergency exit, fire extinguishing gear; and I know the safe endurance with full tanks; to be indicated below for the type of aircraft noted. Type Aircraft Endurance CORNELL 3½ HRS	FEB 8 1944	F. Lawrence Student
Before Flying Solo	I have noted and know where the authorized low flying area and the authorized forced landing field are located at the schools indicated below. E.F.T.S. S.F.T.S.	FEB 8 1944	F. Lawrence Student
Instructors remarks on pupils weaknesses E.F.T.S.			
Before acting as Captain of the aircraft on Mutual Instruction either Instrument or Navigation.	This student has completed a total of not less than 35 hours combined dual and solo flying on the following type of aircraft and is considered a CAPABLE AND RELIABLE PILOT and to qualify as Captain of the aircraft for Mutual Instruction or Mutual Navigation Flights. Type of Aircraft		Squadron Commander
Before acting as Safety Pilot	I have read and fully understood the "Restrictions in the use of the Blind Flying Hood."		Student
Instructors remarks on pupils weaknesses at S.F.T.S.			

Student's log book from No 5 EFTS belonging to "F. Lawrence." Note the requirement that students had to be familiar with designated low flying zones before being allowed to fly solo.

Photo courtesy of the Museum of the Highwood

THE OFFICER'S LOUNGE AT NO 5 EFTS

Photo courtesy of the Museum of Highwood

THE PARKING LOT OF THE COLD LAKE RADAR STATION ATOP RADAR HILL, NOVEMBER 1963.

THE STATION IS NOW HOME TO THE COLD LAKE MUSEUMS

Photo courtesy of the Cold Lake Air Force Museum

THE COLD LAKE RADAR STATION, UNDATED. THE STATION WORKED TO SUPPLEMENT THE PINETREE LINE BUT FUNCTIONED SEPARATELY FROM THE OFFICIAL SERIES OF RADAR STATIONS THAT FORMED THE LINE.

Photo courtesy of Cold Lake Air Force Museum

The Cold Lake Radar Station, undated. The road in the top left corner was the one used for Soapbox Car races.

Photo courtesy of the Cold Lake Air Force Museum

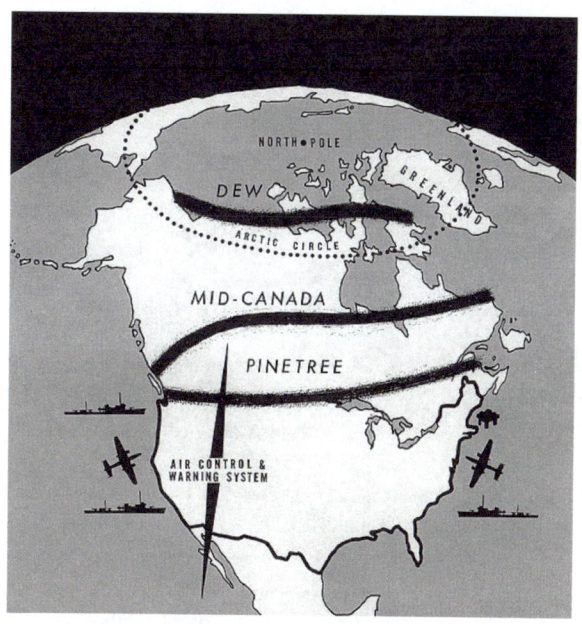

Three radar lines operated in Canada during the Cold War, of which only the Mid-Canada Line officially had a station in Alberta, though other radar stations in the province contributed to Pinetree Line efforts.

THE COLD LAKE RADAR STATION. THOUGH THIS PHOTO IS NOT DATED, NOTE THE FENCE THAT SURROUNDS THE RADAR STATION, WHICH WAS ADDED DUE TO HEIGHTEN SECURITY THREAT LEVELS DURING THE COLD WAR.

Photo courtesy of the Cold Lake Air Force Museum

THE RADAR PERSONNEL TEAM FROM 1968, PICTURED IN FRONT OF ONE OF THE DOMES ON TOP OF RADAR HILL.

PERSONNEL WOULD LIVE WITHIN THE TOWNS OF COLD LAKE OR GRAND CENTRE (PRESENT DAY CITY OF COLD LAKE)

Photo courtesy of the Cold Lake Air Force Museum

A Tim Hortons cup from Kandahar, Afghanistan. Much like the days of the Second World War when the Red Cross shipped boxes of comforts overseas, the tastes of home were provided to soldiers serving in the Afghan conflict.

Photo courtesy of Wanda Stacey

The badge for 418 "City of Edmonton" Squadron, designed by Inuit children being treated for tuberculosis. The motto, an Inuktitut word, means "Defend even unto death."

Photo courtesy of the RCAF Association

The badge of the 401 "Rams" currently based in CFB Cold Lake. Their motto translates to "Very swift death for the enemy."

Photo courtesy of the RCAF Association

Every Squadron created its own badge and adorned it with a motto of their choice. Pictured here is the badge of the 403 "City of Calgary" Squadron, also nicknamed "Wolf."

Photo courtesy of the RCAF Association

The squadron badge for 408 "Goose" Squadron. The goose is not only a symbol of Canada but also known for flying in formations, much like 408 did during the Second World War.

Photo courtesy of the RCAF Association

The 409 "Nighthawk" Squadron chose the cloak in their badge and their motto–"Midnight is our noon"– in honour of their role as night fighters.

Photo courtesy of the RCAF Association

The 417 "City of Windsor" Squadron honoured their North African and Italian campaign involvement with their badge.

Photo courtesy of the RCAF Association

The 410 "Cougar" Squadron motto, "Wandering by night," described their wartime bombing activities.

The squadron also retains their trophy from Soapbox Car racing in Cold Lake.

Photo courtesy of the RCAF Association

Like many Squadrons formed during the war, 419 chose a distinctly Canadian animal as it's badge. Their motto translates to "Beware of the moose."

Photo courtesy of the RCAF Association

Peacetime

Flying Officer Gordon King was still a prisoner in Stalag Luft III by May of 1945. He spent much of the war organising sports teams in the camp–his parents even received special recognition on his behalf from the YMCA for these efforts. In the final days of the war, he was playing a game of hockey to the sound of distant Russian guns: the liberating force was near.

German soldiers evacuated the camp and marched the prisoners north until eventually they realised the cause was lost and decided to give up. Nazi Germany officially surrendered on May 8th, 1945, after six long years of fighting. Flying Officer King spent VE Day in London, England before he returned home and married his childhood sweetheart. The couple moved to Edmonton in 1965 and there are several streets, a pond, and a gate named after him in the Keswick neighbourhood of the city.

Overseas, Canadian troops would remain active for up to a year after the war, aiding in the rebuilding of occupied territories in Europe. Canada was not running the long-term occupation in West Germany, so the size of its military, including the RCAF, decreased dramatically after the war ended. However, many units reformed soon after they were disbanded, as Canada came to terms with a new threat: the Cold War.

The Cold War did not have a singular official beginning, nor did it ever technically become an armed conflict. Immediately following the surrender of Nazi Germany, the alliance between Britain, the United States, and the Union of Soviet Socialist Republics (USSR) began to dissolve. All three forces, as well as France, had decided to maintain an occupying presence in Germany to facilitate post-war recovery, having determined that the rise of Adolf Hitler was largely caused by the severe economic depression Germany had suffered when it was made to pay back immense debts following the Great War (1914-1918). Britain and the United States maintained democratic societies and wanted to instil the same in post-war Germany, while the USSR maintained a communist state and likewise wanted Germany to do the same. These tensions were illustrated at the forming of the United Nations (UN) in 1945 when the USSR, France, Britain, and the United States were all granted permanent seats on the Security Council, only for the USSR to demand that China also be added to the council so it would not be the only communist nation represented. Out of fear that the USSR would grow too powerful, the western powers requested that Berlin, which was situated in Soviet-occupied East Germany, be divided into East Berlin and West Berlin, ensuring that the capital of Germany could be influenced by both democratic and communist ideologies.

In response to this growing unease, the North Atlantic Treaty Organization (NATO) was formed in 1949. This was a treaty between 12 nations (it has now grown to 31 as of 2023 with additional countries expressing interest in joining) that would ensure instant declaration of support if any of the countries in the organization were attacked by Russia. This was particularly important for Canada as the country's northern territories share a sea border with Russia.

Canada had already created the Auxiliary Air Force in 1946. This was a number of reformed squadrons that were intended to train and maintain wartime skills, including the 418 "City of Edmonton" Squadron and the 403 "City of Calgary" Squadron.

403 Squadron–which is (as of 2023) based at CFB Gagetown, New Brunswick–was originally formed in Warwickshire, England in 1941. Adopted by the City of Calgary, the unit flew both offensive and defensive missions in north-west Europe. They were disbanded in Fassburg, Germany in July of 1945, only to be reformed in their adoptive city in 1948. Much like 418 Squadron reforming in Edmonton, this return to their adoptive city was relatively rare. 403 Squadron would remain operational until 1957 when it was redesignated to light transport and emergency rescue, altering its duties away from combat training.

418 Squadron was first reformed at Blatchford field in Edmonton, but in 1958 would move to the Namao base that had been occupied by the USAAF for the duration of the war. There had been serious discussion in making the Namao base the international airport for the Edmonton area, however land south of the city near Leduc was ultimately chosen. Not wanting to waste a world-renowned airport, the Namao base was offered to 418 Squadron instead.

418 did not forget its adoptive city of Edmonton, however. Though the squadron had not had an official badge during the war, they found the need to create one after, when Saint Clement Danes Church in London requested that the 418

badge be placed in their floor. This was done as a thank you for money raised by the squadron after the church was destroyed in the Blitz.

As a way of involving their home city, the squadron opened a design contest to Inuit children who were staying at the Charles Camsell Hospital in Edmonton. Since Edmonton had continued to be a gateway to the territories, healthcare was often provided to remote communities via the city. In the case of tuberculosis (TB) epidemics–which were still common in remote northern communities into the 20th Century– medicine was flown from the Blatchford airport in Edmonton, and, in severe cases, patients were airlifted to Edmonton where the hospital treated them in relative isolation. Patients at the hospital came up with a badge with an Inuk holding a harpoon and standing on an ice-flow. This would be the first RCAF crest to have a human figure on it and, when a motto was suggested by a priest in Churchill, Manitoba, it would be the first squadron to have a motto not in English, French, or Latin. The motto was "Piyautailili", an Inuktitut phrase meaning "Defend even unto death." Combined, this badge and motto represented the intertwined relationship between Edmonton and the territories in cultural and military means. (This closely linked identity is part of the reason why Edmontonians were given the nickname "Eskimos" by their longtime rival city of Calgary. Between 1949 and 2020 the city's football team would bear this nickname. The team's name has since been changed, as the term "eskimo" has been noted as incorrect when referring to the Inuit community.)

For much of its time directly before the move to Namao, 418 upkept wartime skills by sending members for summer training programs that pitted squadrons from across Canada against each other in mock-Soviet invasions. Though there was a great amount of joy taken in both successfully defending or invading a base during the exercises, the fear of a real invasion was great. There was a significant amount of tension growing in the world and the idea that the USSR might send troops over the Arctic Circle into Canada was very present in everyone's minds. This very quickly morphed into another possibility when, in 1949, the USSR successfully detonated its first nuclear bomb. Faux scenarios began to shift focus to tasks such as retreating from the danger zones in the event of a nuclear attack and scouting and mapping destruction to proceed with cleaning up nuclear fallout. Though Canada was at risk of attack, it was thought that the USSR would decide to attack the US first, rather than attack one of its allies and risk full-strength retaliation.

To minimise the potential damage of a nuclear attack, the United States proposed and convinced Canada to agree to a radar system to be built in the country that could detect Soviet planes that might be flying overhead.

Mid-Canada and Pinetree Lines

Construction of the Pinetree Line began in 1951, a joint venture between Canada and the United States. Plans had begun five years earlier, in 1946, but at the time the project was deemed too expensive.

The Pinetree Line consisted of 33 main stations and six "gap fillers." 11 of the main stations were paid for by the RCAF and 16 of them were manned by RCAF staff. Engineers from Canadian National Railway, Canadian Pacific Railway, and Bell Telephone were hired to help with the infrastructure of this massive project.

The Line used "pulse radar" which was, unfortunately, not adept at detecting close-to-the-ground targets. It was also placed too far south, providing only two hours of warning to major cities, which would not be sufficient time to prepare for a nuclear attack, especially since the USSR had jet-powered bombers, which made them even faster than traditional aircraft. This meant the warning time was potentially even shorter. Despite these flaws, however, the Pinetree Line still operated into the late 1950s.

Though there were no official Pinetree Line stations in Alberta, a radar station was constructed at Cold Lake that worked closely with the Line and used similar kinds of radar.

The radar station in Cold Lake was originally built near the town of Grand Centre. Cold Lake proper was much closer to its namesake body of water, but Grand Centre was closer to what became known as "Radar Hill." As the name implies, it is a large hill that would be ideal for a radar station as it is physically above any potential disruptions. The military base, which would be the first flying station constructed in Canada after the Second World War, was situated in the town of Medley. These towns, collectively known as "Tri-Town," have all since amalgamated into the City of Cold Lake.

The radar base was built between 1952 and 1954 and, in 1955, 42 Aircraft Control and Warning Squadron moved in. Their main job was not to search for potential enemy aircraft but to provide radar control for CF-100 interceptors, which were twin-engine all-weather jets that were training in the area. However, if at any point an aircraft failed to identify itself to a control tower, then the base might become the front line of a Soviet invasion.

The Cold Lake base represents far more than just the technical aspects of the air force during the Cold War. The base there was intrinsically connected with the "Tri-Town" area. Though all three towns did exist before the base, the population rose as the air base brought new people into the area and bolstered businesses. This was very similar to how the BCATP had fed the economies of nearby towns, except that this base was much more permanent. Even if the threat of invasion dissipated, there was still a need to control the air space via radar and an expectation to keep pilots up to date with the latest technology.

Cold Lake had previously missed other economic opportunities. There was oil and gas discovered in the area, however the boom of the oil industry never reached town. Aside from tourists visiting the lake itself as well as being a well-known destination for hunting and fishing, there was very little outside of the military base to draw civilians to the area. So, for a long time, much of the population was military personnel and their spouses and children. This did not mean there was no one but the military population there. The area had been home to the small communities of settlers since the 19th Century and a strong Denesųłiné community, referred to as Cold Lake First Nations, occupies reserve land in and around town. However, there was a noticeable uptick in new residents after the base was established.

The Cold Lake military hospital shows the growing number of on-base families through its expansion, families that would have socialised and shopped in the nearby towns. When it opened in 1954, the hospital had 25 beds. Despite seeming like a low number, this actually made it the largest military medical facility west of Ottawa. It was also one of the few military hospitals that provided care for member's dependents (the time, wives counted as dependents as they were usually stay-at-home mothers without their own income.)

Specialists were employed by the base hospital to avoid putting strain on the nearby John Neil Hospital, which served the civilian population in Cold Lake and, like many rural hospitals, was under-staffed. The closest other hospital was in Edmonton, which was over 300km away on gravel roads. By 1959, the Canadian military amalgamated its medical services, giving the base hospital the name Canadian Forces Hospital (CFH) Cold Lake. By this time the hospital had added an operating room, a plastering room for casting broken limbs, 25 more beds, and a nursery to serve the population of military member's wives and their children. This was even before the height of the base later in the Cold War.

Also directly influencing the town of Cold Lake was the CHCL Radio Station, which was started in Medley (a name which the base community still retains). The station began in 1955 as a shortwave radio club playing music to the houses on base. However, more than just Medley heard it and in just ten years it would become a properly recognized radio station, purchasing a 40-Watt transmitter in 1966 to clearly broadcast to the entire Tri-Town area.

In 1969, the year the station got an official office, the recorded wage for a DJ was 50¢/hour ($3.98/hour in 2023), and the station had an annual budget of $3600 ($28,673 in

2023). Employees consisted of one paid employee and one to two volunteers, all generally military members or military dependents.

Similarly, the local newspaper, *The Courier*, was started on base by volunteers. It was a twice monthly publication and it only originally published from 1955 until 1958. However, in Canada's centennial year, the paper was revived and continues to this day–although it is now entirely online.

Churches on base were available in both Roman Catholic and Protestant denominations and they, as well as the base's school, allowed members of the civilian community to attend.

Fun was plentiful on base as well. Members of the Cold Lake radar station took to building Soap Box Cars to race down the steep road of Radar Hill. These were one man cars made out of aluminium, plywood, fibreglass, plastic, or other very light materials. The finished products often only weighed about 66kgs (150lbs). Wheels were bought premade or were taken from other vehicles like bicycles, and brakes were regular friction brakes. The cars would be raced from the top of Radar Hill to the bottom with the different squadrons from the Cold Lake base building and decorating their own vehicles to enter. Generally, cars could reach speeds of between 30 to 50 km/h but the record speed was 164 km/h. (The current posted speed limit on the road, which is now 69 Ave, is 50km/h.)

All of this rapid expansion, all of these new buildings and community projects, was all unfolding in the shadow of the radar station up on Radar Hill. Literally in the shadow of the new technology of the Cold War.

As mentioned, there were no Pinetree Line stations in Alberta, however 3 radar stations that operated within the province are usually identified as being a part of the line. Canadian Forces Station (CFS) Beaverlodge, CFS Penhold, and the station in Cold Lake. This discrepancy likely comes from the fact that additional "filler stations" were added to the Pinetree Line in the hope that this would allow for extra security against potential intruders.

Each station included three large white radar domes in which the actual radar dish operated, protected from rain and snow. One of these would be a height finder, one a medium range search radar, and one a back-up search radar. Depending on how isolated the radar station was, other infrastructure could include libraries, schools, fire stations, and recreational facilities. In the case of a location like Cold Lake, which already had established communities nearby, this was not as necessary as radar personnel were not confined to the base outside of their work shifts.

The Pinetree Line overall was short lived. By 1956 the Mid-Canada Line was under construction. This was built slightly further north than the Pinetree Line not to replace it, but rather to supplement it by providing more than just a few hours of warning in case of attack. Only 8 out of the 98 stations in the Mid-Canada Line were actually manned, the rest being Doppler radar which did not need constant human supervision to run. One of the manned stations was RCAF Stoney Mountain.

Located near the town of Anzac, the station had been a US Army base during the Second World War, though the base required an air strip as there was no other way to get supplies to troops. In 1957, it opened as RCAF Stoney Mountain and began work as a manned Mid-Canada Line station. Being isolated from large population centres, this base required more infrastructure to provide the necessary comforts to radar personnel onsite. The base was not large, however, as it only needed to house enough personnel to keep the radar running and record any activity. The station operated until 1964, just one year before the Mid-Canada Line would be shut down. Following its disbanding, RCAF Stoney Mountain was completely dismantled. The site was used by the forestry service in the 1990s but remains otherwise abandoned.

The reason for the Mid-Canada Line being shut down was the advances made in radar technology. Semi-Automatic Ground Environment (SAGE) systems combined data from multiple stations onto one screen to allow for a more complete and effective radar system. This would result in the creation of the Distance Early Warning (DEW) Line in the Arctic region of Canada, which gave more than ample warning time in case of nuclear attack compared to previous warning systems. Despite this new technology rendering the Mid-Canada Line obsolete, several Pinetree Line stations (or similar stations such as Cold Lake) remained operational until the end of the Cold War in 1991.

Even after the DEW Line was constructed, Edmonton remained in its position as gateway to the North. Being one of the northernmost airports not in the territories, Blatchford Airfield was a final stop for supplies and radar crew members before they headed up into the remote regions of the Arctic, as well as being a busy hub of commercial air travel. This was part of the reason 418 Squadron eventually sought to move to their own base, as the Blatchford airfield was incredibly busy.

Changes to the Air Force

Up until the 1960s, the three branches of the Canadian military operated separately. The Army, Air Force, and Navy naturally functioned in different realms and though they did help each other out quite often, especially in times of war, their management and administration was independent of one another.

This changed in 1964 when the process of unification began. Over the course of four years, all three branches would become a part of the Canadian Armed Forces (CAF). Part of this was renaming all current stations. RCAF Station Cold Lake, for example, was renamed Canadian Forces Base (CFB) Cold Lake. This was the same in Namao.

In Cold Lake, the base remained entirely occupied by the air force, but in Namao the base was transferred between a variety of Commands between 1968 and 1994, when it was officially handed over to the Canadian Army. This did not mean that the air force had to vacate their place there, but rather that the base was under army control with the air force also occupying the same space, an arrangement that continues to this day.

Unification also moved the headquarters of the Air Force to Ottawa, now shared with the Army and Navy, and altered the uniforms so they were all much similar.

As the Cold War continued across the globe, Canada was called to play a more active role in the potential conflict. This began by addressing the large number of both Soviet but also American planes that were flying over Canada's Arctic region. From the beginning, the role of the Air Force was to give Canada control over its own air space, and by the Cold War there were fears that this had not been realised.

The United States Air Force (USAF, previously USAAF) had, by the early 1970s, done more to map out and photograph the remote Arctic regions of Canada than the Canadian government had. As well, knowing that enemy planes were flying over one's own skies when you were hosting a radar system specifically to deter them could reflect very poorly on the country. This was also causing the Soviet government to question Canada's claim to the Arctic region.

This questioned claim goes back to the 17th Century, when the Hudson's Bay Company signed a charter with the British government, giving them sovereignty over all the land where the water flowed into the Hudson Bay. This was assumed to include any remote Arctic regions, though it was later understood that most of the modern-day Yukon, Nunavut, and North-West Territories are actually in the Arctic Ocean watershed. This region was almost exclusively inhabited by the Inuit, none of whom ever signed formal treaties with the Canadian Government, meaning that it could be argued that the government had limited or even no control over the land as the people living there had never formally agreed to share it.

As the Soviets flew over the areas, they argued that they had "discovered" much of the land before the Canadians and therefore could claim ownership of it. (This did ignore the Inuit rights to their ancestral home; however, the fear was not that the USSR would work with the Inuit to take the land from Canada, but rather they would invade and colonise it as other countries had done before. This would create a Soviet foothold on the North American continent, one that would likely extend south of the DEW Line, rendering the front-line detection and defence system completely useless.)

In response to these fears, 418 Squadron was sent to the Arctic. Based out of Norman Wells, North-West Territories, the squadron focused on mapping out air strips that had been built by oil and mining companies and completing an approximate census of Indigenous communities. They would also scout abandoned DEW Line stations to ensure they were not being pillaged or used as bases for invading armies as well as being tasked with enforcing pollution laws on oil companies operating up north.

At CFB Cold Lake, there was a focus on technological advancements. As early as 1950, Canada had offered itself up as a place to train NATO pilots. Harkening back to the days of the BCATP, Canada had lots of open space and knew that towns would readily accept the booms in business that came with an air base being built nearby. Though the NATO training plan only lasted until 1958, it saw over 5,000 pilots from all around the world graduate from the program. These pilots were then deployed into Europe, where countries were still aiding with reconstruction efforts following the Second World War, including attempting to lift the Iron Curtain that the USSR had draped across the borders of East and West Germany. Unlike during the Second World War, however, RCAF members deployed to Europe during the Cold War were allowed to bring their families.

Even after the original NATO training plan had ended, Cold Lake continued to be an important part of training efforts. By the late 1950s, all CF-100 jets were consolidated at Cold Lake for training. In accordance with NATO standard, squadrons deployed to a weapons range in Morocco or Sardinia twice a year to practise air gunnery. Before these large international training camps, initial training and upkeep of skills would be done on a domestic scale in places like Cold Lake, which boasted its own weapons range.

Cold Lake's radar station was updated to use SAGE radar in 1962, the same year that Fidel Castro signed a deal to allow the USSR to build nuclear launch facilities in Cuba. This deal meant that the Soviets had nuclear weapons within easy striking distance of the United States for the first time without having to pass over Canada and the radar warning systems in place there. There was a thirteen-day period, known as the Cuban Missile Crisis, in which the Cold War was very likely to heat up as government officials from all sides scrambled to negotiate a way to avoid nuclear war. Eventually it was decided that the USSR would remove all their nuclear weapons from Cuba in exchange for the United States doing the same in Turkey.

In response to this near miss, Cold Lake was selected to train Canadian pilots on CF-104 *Starfighter* aircraft, which could deploy nuclear weapons if the need arose. To facilitate the training, 417 Squadron was reformed at Cold Lake, now being called a Strike and Reconnaissance Operational Training Unit. These training courses involved eighty hours of both flying and ground school courses both about the aircraft and about nuclear delivery. It also meant that pupils and ground crew all had to undergo high-level security clearance to work with nuclear weapons.

It is interesting to note that all nuclear weapons in Canada at the time were on loan from the United States, meaning that Canada did not actually have any say as to when they were deployed. However, given the country's position between the United States and Russia (neighbouring the latter across the Arctic Sea) it was imperative that the Canadian air force know how to work with, deploy, and respond to nuclear weapons.

As the threat of nuclear attack mounted, the Canadian government was actively encouraging its citizens to build nuclear fallout shelters. These shelters were not very common in Canada compared to the United States. Here they were thought to be far too expensive for the common man and many Canadians felt that the chance of survival in the case of a nuclear war was too low to bother with such pricey precautionary measures.

Nuclear Weaponry in Alberta

Throughout the 1970s, training for the RCAF began to focus on the potential need to deploy nuclear weapons. Cold Lake added several new squadrons to its base, all of whom focused either on training pilots or testing nuclear innovation. In 1971 the Aerospace Engineering Test Establishment (AETE) was created in Cold Lake with the aim of conducting flight evaluations including being one of the places where pilots were trained on new aircrafts.

By the 1980s, *Starfighters* were phased out of use, being replaced with CF-18 *Hornets*. The *Hornets* were such an important technological advancement for the military that they were eagerly shown off in airshows. They became so popular, in fact, that crew members and individual planes would be selected to spend a season just performing in the air show circuit. To keep up with the jets there were also advancements on the ground at CFB Cold Lake as a new flight simulator, supply warehouse, weapons systems trainer, engine bay, and other range improvements had to be constructed to keep the facilities up to date.

All these advancements were needed, as Cold Lake would soon be chosen as one of the testing grounds for the new cruise missile technology.

The cruise missile was a controversial advancement in nuclear weaponry. The design of the missiles were a successor to the V-1 bombs that 418 Squadron had famously fought during the Second World War. Like the V-1s they were autonomous, meaning they could be launched alone instead of dropped by a plane (initial tests did have them dropped from bomber aircraft). Cruise missiles were jet propelled like the V-1s, but technological advancements made them much faster and able to be launched from as far as 2400 km away from their intended target. Each missile had a flight computer tied to a GPS system and terrain following radar. These advancements allowed the missile to enter enemy territory without being detected by radar and be called back from its attack if something were to go wrong.

Though no live nuclear cargo was carried on each bomb during testing, the empty bombs were deployed over the weapons range in Cold Lake, being escorted by the *Hornets* into the range and then parachuting to the ground. Generally, each bomb landed within a few feet of the target, indicating they were very accurate weapons–though one did accidentally overshoot and fall through thin ice on the nearby lake. Testing costs, including the fuel needed for the *Hornets* escorting the missiles, were all covered by the United States as they were still the owners of all the nuclear weaponry that would be placed in the missiles if they were ever dropped for real.

The cruise missile was one of the first nuclear weapons in Canada that was considered offensive. Up until that point, most Cold War related efforts in the country were defensive– such as radar warning systems, training of pilots for reconnaissance missions, NATO training plans to defend Europe against Russian expansion–now, for the first time since the Second World War, Canada was training its pilots to attack.

There had been many rallies and marches around the country to protest nuclear weaponry, but by the early 1980s eyes were on Cold Lake for the first time. The widely hated weapon was being tested right in Alberta, and plenty of people had something to say about it.

A slew of protestors flooded into Cold Lake. The highway into the weapons range where testing was taking place was barricaded and there were vigils being held in Grand Centre. Some townspeople resented the protestors' presence, others joined in on the actions themselves. A local church even allowed visiting protestors to stay in the basement while they were in town.

The RCAF had anticipated this level of response, however. In 1982, just one year prior to the first cruise missile testing, a fence had been installed around the radar station on Radar Hill to provide a new level of security of the facility. Prior to that point, the station had been relatively accessible to the public aside from actual entry into the buildings. Security was heightened again in 1983 when it was discovered that Direct Action intended to target CFB Cold Lake.

Direct Action, also known as the "Squamish Five" were a group of activists who used more aggressive guerilla tactics to promote their anti-nuclear (and therefore anti-cruise missile), pro-environment, and anti-pornography stance. In the early 1980s they vandalised BC's Ministry of the Environment, bombed the Dunsmuir Hydro station in BC, and then drove to Ontario to bomb the Litton Industries building in Rexdale, which was supplying electronics for cruise missile guidance systems. Though the group did issue warnings before the bombings and take full credit for their work, they were not caught until after they had rebranded as the "Wimmin's Fire Brigade" and bombed a series of Red Hot Video stores in Vancouver (all of which sold pornographic films). During this time, it was discovered that CFB Cold Lake was one of their intended targets. Allegedly, they were planning on filling a truck with explosives and driving it out onto the flight line before detonating it.

The group was arrested in Vancouver in January 1983 and underwent a very public trial, which included a punk band releasing a charity single to raise money to pay the group's legal fees. In the end all five were convicted and received various prison sentences. Several have since been released.

In 1985 members of Greenpeace–another environmental activist group–set up in Wandering River with plans to deploy a net, held up by weather balloons, to catch a cruise missile in the air. There were two nets launched, one on January 15 and a second on February 19. Both were 100 feet across and decorated with anti-nuclear banners. The first net failed to launch on time but the second came within 75 feet of the missile. This nearly intercepted missile was the first free flight cruise missile launched and the first missile fired by the United States Strategic Air Command over a foreign country, being that it was being fired over civilian airspace and not just the weapons range (its intended landing area was within the weapons range). Ironically, the net helped to prove that the missile was able to detect and avoid an obstacle while in flight.

There was another man, around the same time, who intended to launch a large balloon covered in radar reflective materials to interfere with another test. However, RCMP and Transport Canada intervened and convinced him to stop this action.

By 1985 there were recovery efforts underway to retrieve the free flight missiles from the testing area. Each missile had a parachute inside it–tucked into the area where the nuclear warheads would be if the missile was armed–to lower the spent missile to the ground. If actually deployed it would drop the nuclear warhead and continue on, however the tests needed to be more controlled, not only to avoid potentially damaging property outside of the weapons range, but also so the missiles could be retrieved and studied to see if there were any improvements needed.

Cruise missile testing continued until 1994 when Cold Lake hosted the final ever cruise missile test to be launched over Canada. By 1994, testing was being carried out on a cruise missile known as a "Global Shadow" which was a stealth variety of the same weapon. These missiles could not accommodate a parachute, so missiles had to "crash" into the testing range. Because they were stealth missiles, they had to be covered in aluminium material otherwise the aircrafts escorting and intercepting the missile during training would be unable to see it on radar.

Testing continued to be controversial. In the case of the Global Shadow cruise missile, the missile had been made operational 2 years before they even began testing it on Canadian soil, leading many to question why it was being tested at all. There were several theories as to this, including the benefit of having the United States paying for fuel for the escorting aircrafts and the ongoing agreements that the United States and Canada had regarding nuclear testing. However, after 1994, cruise missile testing within the country of Canada ceased.

Canadians Overseas after the Second World War

The first time Canadians deployed overseas in a combat role following the Second World War was the Korean War (1950-1953). This war was the result of tensions between the newly split North and South Koreas, the former of which was being supported by communist Russia and China and the latter wanting to keep a democratic government. Having not been as involved in the war in the Pacific during the 1940s, Canada was also not as heavily involved in the Korean War as compared to the United States. Following the Korean War, Canada was not involved in overseas combat until the Gulf War in 1990/1991.

So named for taking place in the Persian Gulf region, the Gulf War began when Iraq invaded the neighbouring country of Kuwait, gaining control of one of the largest oil reserves in the world. Canadians were first deployed in a combat role to help push the Iraqi forces out of the country but remained in the region as peacekeepers and embargo enforcement for some time after the conflict was resolved.

The initial invasion had been outwardly condemned by the UN, which prompted the United States to rally 35 countries together to counterattack, the largest joint military effort since the Second World War. This was the first time that RCAF fighter pilots worked with Royal Canadian Navy (RCN) units during a combat mission. Previously, RCAF fighters had almost exclusively flown over land or close to shore as flying over open ocean is considered highly dangerous, even today. There were off-the-coast patrols that took place, especially when working in the Arctic regions with mapping efforts, but those were not done by fighter pilots. During the Gulf War the main tactic being used by the 35-country coalition was a naval blockade and present in the air over the blockade was 416 Squadron, which was based out of CFB Cold Lake at the time.

Prior to the invasion of Kuwait, there had been fear of rising tensions at CFB Cold Lake because of its proximity to Cold Lake First Nations. Just months before the invasion overseas, the Canadian military had been sent to Oka, Quebec to disperse a roadblock on a Mohawk reserve that was attempting to stop the expansion of a golf course into their traditional burial grounds. Just after the standoff–now known as the Oka Crisis–began, a rail bridge into CFB Cold Lake caught fire, temporarily cutting the base off from its fuel supplies. It was thought, at the time, that this might be the beginning of a potential standoff in Cold Lake, however all concerns were forgotten when squadrons at the base suddenly found themselves preparing for overseas combat for the first time in nearly 40 years. (The Oka Crisis would come to a resolution just one month after the start of the Gulf War and did not spill over into the Cold Lake area.)

Canada had been known as a Peacekeeping force since the 1950s, however this became the main focus of the CAF following the Gulf War.

In 1992, the UN put together the United Nations Protection Force, which was to be deployed to the former state of Yugoslavia in the Balkan region, which was breaking into multiple smaller countries. Much like the RCAF, Yugoslavia had formed following the First World War and undergone many changes in the interim period. From 1945 until 1991 the country was under communist rule, though not as a part of the Soviet Union. Through the 1980s, the communist government slowly weakened and destabilised, both because of the weakening role of communism on a global scale and because the individual ethnic and religious pockets within the country were beginning to push to become their own nations. In 1991, Slovenia and Croatia declared their independence from the Socialist Federal Republic of Yugoslavia, prompting the beginning of a civil war in the Balkans.

For the first four years of the conflict, Canada's contribution would be mostly infantry based, which was in line with the UN's strategy in the region. In 1995, after the Protection Force mandate expired, NATO took over many of the efforts in the area, which now included having troops in the nations of Macedonia and Bosnia-Herzegovina. It was around this time that 408 Squadron became more directly involved in the conflict.

---

408 Squadron, as mentioned previously, was formed in 1941 in Yorkshire, England. Nicknamed "Goose" because of its mascot,

it was originally adopted by Kingsville, Ontario and disbanded in 1945 in Nova Scotia. It was reformed in Rockcliffe, Ontario in 1949, with members of the squadron would be sent north to map Canada's Arctic region to aid in strengthening Canada's claim to the Arctic. As the region became adequately scouted, the Squadron was moved to Rivers, Manitoba in April of 1964.

In 1971 the Squadron was reformed again. Now part of the unified CAF, the Squadron was to be a Tactical Helicopter Squadron based out of CFB Edmonton, also referred to as CFB Namao. By this time the 418 "City of Edmonton" Squadron had been sent up north to Norman Wells, which left a position open for 408 to provide air support to the 3rd Canadian Division (Army).

Still based out of Edmonton today, 408 Squadron was deployed by NATO to provide air support in the Balkan states, specifically within Kosovo in 1999. The conflict in Kosovo was the result of Serbian and Albanian forces fighting within the region following the now seven years of unrest in the former Yugoslavia. Serbian forces were attempting to drive out ethnic Albanians from the region, prompting NATO to issue a warning that if a ceasefire was not signed, outside military forces would take action. This ceasefire died in negotiations and NATO decided the best course of action was an air-based bombing campaign–different from previous UN efforts in the region which focussed on infantry involvement. Though there were plans to deploy ground troops, the bombing campaign was successful in pushing Serbian forces to accept a ceasefire in June of 1999.

This did not end the Canadian presence in Kosovo, however, as CAF members remained in the country as peacekeepers between December of 1999 and June of 2000.

Though the situation in the Balkan states is far more stable today, Canadian troops are still present in the area to ensure lasting peace and security.

This was not the first deployment for 408 since the squadron had completed its service in the Second World War. The Squadron had been sent to Quebec to provide support during the Oka Crisis (which is likely part of why they were not involved in the Gulf War) in 1991 and was a part of the peacekeeping efforts in Haiti between 1995 and 1997.

Canadian troops had been present in Haiti since 1989, following the dissolution of a dictatorship that had been in control of the country since 1957. In early years, Canadian troops were purely delivering humanitarian aid. After a new president was democratically elected in 1990 and overthrown in a coup a year later, the UN decided to create a stabilisation mission to help restore democracy in the country.

In 1996, Major John King of 408 Squadron was deployed to Haiti for a period of 6 months. King had received his wings in 1987 and worked in Moose Jaw as a flying instructor before being transferred to North Bay, Ontario with the 414 Squadron. A Winnipeg native, King was with 414 when they were moved to Comox, BC but was posted to 408 Squadron at CFB Edmonton in 1994, just two years before his deployment to Haiti.

At the time of the UN mission into Haiti, the country did not have reliable road systems, with roads washing out in frequent heavy rainstorms and the lack of stable government curbing the ability to repair them. This meant the RCAF and other UN countries' air forces, became invaluable to the stabilisation efforts as they were the main source of transportation throughout the country.

The mission in Haiti was not for combat. There were problems with gang violence in urban areas, and soldiers were expected to carry weapons with them if they were leaving their secure base, but two or more soldiers could safely drive to areas of Port-au-Prince to enjoy dinners at the local restaurants and even a round of golf at the local golf course. This relative peace led to many soldiers giving their deployments the tongue-in-cheek name "the Haitian Vacation."

408 Squadron members were flying CH-134 "Twin Huey" helicopters in the country. Haiti is a very mountainous nation, meaning that regular planes would struggle to take off and land amongst the hills. As such, helicopters were a simple and effective way to move people about.

Stabilisation efforts included a lot of construction efforts around the country. Often 408 members were ferrying engineers and building supplies into remote villages to build things like schools that these villages were lacking. The challenge offered to the engineers was that all the building materials must be able to be carried by helicopter, once leading to a school being made out of bricks that almost resembled pieces of LEGO bricks, none of which were more than about eight feet in length. Major King helped move the materials and a team of engineers in one day and by the next picked them up near the newly constructed school building. Communication towers were often looted for valuable supplies such as copper wire and batteries so helicopter pilots would help get repairmen out to restore the towers.

Another crucial part of the mission was medical evacuations (referred to as medevacs). Pilots were placed on call for medevacs for a period of 5 days, during which time they were to stay on base and be ready to run to a helicopter at a moment's notice. However, in keeping with the relatively slow and nonviolent nature of the deployment, King recalled that many times these five days passed with only one call, if even that.

It was only during medevacs that the Canadians ever worked directly with the USAF. Otherwise, there were other countries that worked much more closely with the RCAF. In particular, the Pakistan Armed Forces often coordinated missions with Canadian troops. According to Major King, Pakistan's kitchen staff also always packed extra lunch supplies for any RCAF members out on a mission with them and often invited the Canadians over to their dining facilities for dinner.

One of the toughest challenges for soldiers was the exposure to tropical illnesses. Several members of 408, King included, suffered from bouts of dysentery–which had been considered a life ending illness a century earlier but was by then treatable by drinking plenty of fluids, maintaining hygiene, and, in more severe cases, antibiotics. Some servicemen also suffered from Dengue Fever, which is a virus spread by mosquitoes. Any member of the UN mission was required to take malaria medication to prevent a much more deadly mosquito-based disease, though an unfortunate side effect of the medication was vivid dreams that often turned to nightmares. King also contracted shingles, despite being only thirty years of age when deployed, likely because his immune system was occupied with fighting off other illnesses.

Communication back home was much better than in the days of the Second World War. Instead of waiting weeks or even months for a letter to arrive, hoping it had not been sunk if the mail ship ran into trouble, one member of the squadron oversaw sending and receiving emails. Once a week all emails being sent to 408 members would be printed out and distributed and then replies collected and sent back home. Major King's wife, Carrie, who remained at home in Edmonton, did not have a home computer and so drove to a friend's house to read and reply to her husband's emails once a week. There were also phones available to service members, though calls were limited to fifteen minutes once a week. Once the fifteen minutes was up, the line would go dead.

Canadian troops would remain in Haiti throughout the early 2000s to support the country through more incidents of political unrest. They would again be called to the country in 2010 for humanitarian aid after a devastating earthquake crumbled major population centres. This response would last several years, and Canadian military personnel continue to provide support to Haiti even today.

―――

Also in 1997, members of 408 Squadron who were not over in Haiti were sent to Winnipeg, where a devastating flood required six hundred CAF personnel to descend upon the area, aiding with evacuations, sandbagging efforts to save homes and infrastructure, and rescue efforts. Interestingly, the response to the Red River Flood of 1997 was the biggest Canadian military endeavour since the Second World War. Though Canada had been involved in the Gulf War, which was internationally the largest military campaign since 1945, the number of troops Canada provided was much smaller than the number responding to the flood.

2001 and Onwards

On September 11th, 2001, a group of al-Qaeda affiliated terrorists boarded four commercial airlines in the United States, crashing two of them into the World Trade Centres in New York City. As a result of this attack, all flights in North America were grounded for two days, including military aircrafts.

Following the attacks, which became known as "9/11", the United States launched a campaign to overthrow the Taliban regime in Afghanistan. Though al-Qaeda, a different group led by Osama bin Laden, was believed to be responsible for the attacks, the Taliban were sheltering the terrorist organisation's leader. In October of 2001, just one month after the attacks, Canada officially pledged its support to the United States in their mission and by December of the same year the first Canadians had been deployed.

The Canadian troops were largely based in Kandahar, which was the centre of the multinational mission. Once again, the RCAF was providing helicopter pilots for the mission, as the helicopters would be better suited to the landscape of the country and the need to land in areas without proper runways.

It was not always easy flying, however. In 2011, Lieutenant-Colonel Alexia Hannam was deployed to Afghanistan in the final combat tour by Canadians. With 408 Squadron, Hannam would fly in a total of 48 combat missions. Each mission required two CH-146 "Griffon" helicopters to accompany the CH-47 "Chinook" helicopters, the former of which were armed with machine guns as a defensive measure. Hannam flew Chinook helicopters, and each mission took about a week of planning to safely drop off soldiers and supplies to unprepared landing areas. Again, this was the advantage of helicopters as planes require long runaways for both take-off and landing, whereas helicopters can be put down in sometimes precarious areas.

One precarious area was a dry riverbed that Hannam had to land in while flying in the very early hours of the morning on May 16, 2011. During landing, the helicopter experienced what is called a brown out. This is when enough dust is kicked up by the downwash of the helicopter blades that the dry desert soil blocks visibility during landing. The ground was softer than anticipated and when the Chinook helicopter drifted slightly it dug into the ground and rolled. Because the soldiers being dropped off on the mission were already in their gear (drop offs were quick to avoid enemy mortars being able to take aim at a landed aircraft) no one was wearing any seatbelts, which caused several crush injuries including a broken collar bone and a bruised lung. There was also some shrapnel shot into the cabin during the crash but luckily it did not hit anyone. To put into perspective, night vision goggles are designed to pop off in case of emergency (similar to how ski boots release the ski when someone crashes on a run) and the crash was not severe enough to cause this: all night vision goggles remained atop the soldiers' helmets. The crash did write off the helicopter, however, and an American helicopter that arrived to pick up the worst injuries also struggled to land in the same area. This meant the crash was considered severe, but the injuries were luckily not fatal.

The saving grace of this crash may have been that Hannam was an experienced pilot at the time of her deployment. She had, by then, been in the military for ten years, joining at 18 years old in 2001 because of her interest in being a pilot. The civil route of aviation is quite pricey as many companies require you to have flying experience before you can be paid to fly, and the military offered the opportunity to learn on the job. Hannam also took advantage of the Royal Military College, which allows students to attend university in exchange for military service. She earned a degree in psychology before being posted to 408 Squadron for a total of seven years.

Hannam was on board for the last airborne combat mission that the RCAF deployed in Afghanistan. As it was known ahead of time that this was to be the last of its kind, this ended up being a much larger mission in partnership with American troops since everyone wanted a slice of the action.

Following this final mission, Canada would declare that its combat role in Afghanistan had concluded, and the focus was now on aiding the Afghan government with recovery and ensuring its ability to maintain its own country's security going forward. Canadian troops would remain in the country until March of 2014.

———

On the home front, life has changed a lot of military members and their families. Gone are the days of sprawling BCATP schools and young men far away from home and family. Bases still provide housing as needed, but many families choose to live off base as well-meaning military brats are not confined to just the experience of the military base.

"Military brats" or "base brats"is the nickname given to children of CAF service members. The term does not denote the attitude of the children of military families. Rather it was coined as a way of describing children who are often moved from place to place, experiencing, and absorbing different cultural and regional customs, attitudes, opinions, and even language or accents over their lives.

In a post-COVID pandemic world, this phenomenon may be changing as well, however. Remote work was introduced and adjusted throughout the COVID-19 Pandemic (2020-2023) and showed that not every new list of duties needed to come with a physical move. Some do, of course, but there is a new, and slightly unusual, sense of stability and stillness for a military family that is unique to previous generations.

The military has also seen plenty of changes over the years. Lieutenant-Colonel Hannam, who is currently serving as the Deputy Wing Commander in CFB Cold Lake, has seen many of them even in her time in the RCAF.

Much like its Cold War days, the now seventy-year-old CFB Cold Lake is still intrinsically tied with the surrounding community. At present (2023), about ⅓ of the population of the City of Cold Lake are military members or their dependents. Hannam has also seen an increase in community events that the base personnel have been involved with, herself having worked with Casino Dene on Cold Lake 149 reserve for an event to honour and raise awareness about Missing and

Murdered Indigenous Women and Girls and partnered with the City of Cold Lake for a drag show.

On base, Hannam has seen a push to make spaces more welcoming and inclusive. There are Employee Equity Defence Groups run by military personnel to help identify and remove obstacles that minority groups–such as disabled persons, Indigenous service members, women, members of a visible minority, and LGBTQ+ personnel–face on base. Examples include maternity uniforms for expecting mothers and lactation rooms being made available on the bases, the latter of which Hannam got to use herself after the birth of her son.

There has also been a push to have a Military Families Resource Centre (MFRC) available on every base. The MFRC provides support to military families in the form of community events like paint night and other fundraising endeavours, it also ensures that if a military spouse is alone while their partner is on deployment, there is someone to check in on them and ensure they are coping with the deployment. These check-ups are also to see if they need help with household tasks like shovelling the driveway in the winter. This is to help make deployments less stressful on spouses and children and is considered part of the work duties for selected squadron members. Real tangible changes like this have been a great moral booster and pushed the military into the modern age.

The role that CFB Cold Lake plays within military duties has also changed with the times once more. No longer is the station needed as a defence against Soviet invasion, but the base still boasts a renowned training ground for NATO air force personnel. Starting in 1978, CFB Cold Lake hosts an annual six-week air combat exercise that sees soldiers from both NATO nations and other non-member nations arrive to train. The aptly named Exercise Maple Leaf offers all these different nations the chance to complete exercises that many are unable to do in their densely populated home countries, once again using the open space that Alberta has to offer. These training duties are only shared with one other location in Canada: the training school at CFB Moose Jaw, Saskatchewan.

CFB Cold Lake also functions as a base for search and rescue missions. The model for search and rescue missions dates back to the BCATP and Wop May. His efforts to create a dedicated search and rescue unit live on in the form of Search and Rescue (SAR).

As of 1951, medical staff were being trained to parachute into rescue sites to provide medical assistance in remote or hard to access areas. These RCAF medics included five nursing sisters, who were the first female officers of any service to wear aerial operations badges, which were issued to qualified "Para Rescue" personnel. The term Para Rescue was replaced with SAR in 1957 as not every mission required a parachute.

Through the 1960s and 1970s, these rescue missions became more important as there was an increase in civilian aviation and more flights heading up to Arctic regions. Today, Cold Lake only sees between five and fifteen rescue missions in a year, but other larger bases see multiple in a week.

Into The Future

It is a thirty-five-minute drive from the edge of the City of Calgary to the turn off towards Morley. As it is situated on the Stoney 142/143/144 Reserve, the community is also referred to as Mînî Thnî and contains all the essentials for a prairie town: two schools, a church, a pharmacy, a Subway, and a hockey arena. There are no traces left of the air station that stood near the Canadian Pacific Railway tracks for a brief period in 1920 and 1921. The temporary hangars are long gone, and the runway undetectable.

———

Over an hour south-east of Morely, the No 5 Elementary Flying Training School is now the High River Regional Airport. The layout is the same as it was during the British Commonwealth Air Training Plan but even though the 187 Royal Canadian Air Cadets still meet there, it is no longer a military establishment. Just north of the site the town thrives as a farming community, most famous for its appearances on the small screen, having been a filming location for the CBC soap opera *Heartland* (2007-present) and HBO's *The Last of Us* (2023-present).

Into The Future

Travelling north to Calgary, the former No 1 Repair Depot, where all planes used in the west during the British Commonwealth Air Training Plan would pass through when in need, is completely erased, replaced with suburbs. At the junction of Crowchild and Glenmore Trails there is no indication of the aviation history that was made in that spot.

Blatchford Field, a hub of transportation during and after the Second World War, is now the future home of the Blatchford housing project within the City of Edmonton. The Alberta Aviation Museum and 700 "City of Edmonton" Wing of the Royal Canadian Air Force Association occupies the historic Hangar 14, built during the Second World War, and there are plans to restore and renovate Hangar 11 to give the building new life. The runways have been torn up; the tower has gone quiet. Just across the street, hotels and strip malls creep in, the city slowly taking over.

Atop Radar Hill in Cold Lake, over 300 kilometres north-east of Edmonton, the radar station no longer searches the skies for invading planes. Instead, it houses the Cold Lake Museums, which cover the military, civilian, and Indigenous history of the area in three distinct galleries. The long road up to it, once a racetrack for soapbox cars, now sees only museum goers. The fence, put up sixty years ago to protect against the security threat of anti-nuclear protests, now ensures that artefacts are safe during the off season.

Across the province, the cracked tarmac and fallen down hangars of Alberta's aviation past wait, hidden in plain sight, for someone to notice them, to see them again. But they are not the sign of the end for the RCAF in Alberta. Even 100 years after the first station received its title, after the Bessonneau hangers and radar towers and tactical helicopters, the skies above Cold Lake still ring with the roar of jets. Helicopters still faithfully follow the river when they fly north of Edmonton, the steady thump of their rotors unmistakable. Like the first airmen who took to the skies, training for a mission that was bigger than themselves, securing a future in the air, the RCAF still remains today, changing hats as it needs to: Training Grounds, War Heroes, Radar Defence Lines, Air Transport, Peacekeepers, Search and Rescue.

Royal Canadian Air Force.

Author's Note and Acknowledgments

Writing about military history has always been something I have run into while running away from it. Being a military kid myself, growing up with moving boxes and Remembrance Day services as a staple in my life, I scrambled to find other things to learn about. However, the military always seemed to find me again and again no matter how much I tried to avoid it.

And it's a good thing too. As I found out while writing this, there was still so much about the RCAF that I didn't know. I spent a year peeling back layers and layers of history that had always been right there, but that I had never properly looked at before. And even with a year's worth of effort, I am sure that I have barely scratched the surface of many of the topics here. My hope with this book is that it will inspire others to take the time to look deeper, to stop at the places mentioned the next time they're passing through and spend some time diving into the rich history of military aviation that Alberta has to offer.

Of course, I must also take the time to properly acknowledge all of the wonderful people and places that I was able to get to know while researching and writing.

Thank you so much to the Cold Lake Museums, particularly curator Wanda Stacey, who not only provided me with a wealth of knowledge but also became a starting point for this very daunting research task.

The Museum of the Highwood in High River was also an invaluable source of information. Thank you to Sam Locken for your time and effort in gathering so many sources and photographs for me to look through, you helped lay the perfect foundation to tell this story.

Also, a big thank you to Lieutenant-Colonel Alexia Hannam and Major John King for allowing me to interview each of you about your experiences in the military. Without firsthand accounts like yours, a history like this would feel frail at best.

I'd also like to give a special thanks to my friends and family, many of whom politely wandered behind me during my many museum visits or sat with me as I fretted over how to explain all of this on paper.

And of course, thank you so much to the 700 Wing RCAF Association for this opportunity. Thank you for trusting me to write this history that I know you all hold so near and dear. Hopefully I touched on at least half the topics that you wanted me to.

Bibliography

"4 Wing History." Government of Canada. March 16, 2021. https://www.canada.ca/en/air-force/corporate/wings/4-wing/history.html

"25 Years Ago: Combat and Cold Lake." Originally from *The Courier,* January 19, 2016. Reprinted with permission by the Government of Canada, February 26, 2016. https://www.canada.ca/en/department-national-defence/maple-leaf/rcaf/migration/2016/25-years-ago-combat-and-cold-lake.html

"About Pinetree Line." Civil Defense Museum. Accessed June 1, 2023. http://civildefencemuseum.ca/about-pinetree-line

"About Us." Cold Lake First Nations. https://clfns.com/about-us/

"Afghanistan, 2001-2014." Veterans Affairs Canada. Last edited May 20, 2022. https://www.veterans.gc.ca/eng/remembrance/wars-and-conflicts/afghanistan/

Alberta Aviation Museum. Edmonton, Alberta. Visited June 18, 2023.

"Balkans, 1991-Present." Veterans Affairs Canada. Last edited February 22, 2023. https://www.veterans.gc.ca/eng/remembrance/wars-and-conflicts/caf-operations/balkans

Birell, Dave. *The Canadian Air Force at High River.* Nanton, Alberta: The Nanton Lancaster Society, 2019.

"Birkland, Henry." Second World War Service Records– War Dead, 1939-1947. Government of Canada. https://recherche-collection-search.bac-lac.gc.ca/eng/home/record?app=kia&IdNumber=2798&q=Birkland

Boileau, John. "Arthur Roy Brown." The Canadian Encyclopedia. May 26, 2008. Last edited March 18, 2021. https://www.thecanadianencyclopedia.ca/en/article/arthur-roy-brown

Bomber Command Museum of Canada. Nanton, Alberta. Visited August 10, 2023.

"British Commonwealth Air Training Plan." Bomber Command Museum of Canada. https://www.bombercommandmuseum.ca/bcatp/british-commonwealth-air-training-plan-in-alberta/

Brogan, D.W. *Behind the Glory: Canada's Role in the Allied Air War*. Toronto: Thomas Allen, 2005.

Butts, Edward. "Wop May." The Canadian Encyclopedia. May, 2008. Last edited January, 2019. https://www.thecanadianencyclopedia.ca/en/article/wilfrid-reid-may

"Canada's Radar Line." The Secrets of Radar Museum. Accessed June 1, 2023. https://militarybruce.com/abandoned-canadian-military-bases/the-mid-canada-line/

Cold Lake Museums. Cold Lake Alberta. Specifically the Cold Lake Air Force Museum. Visited August 8th, 2023.

"Cold Lake- Population." Government of Canada. Last edited February 28, 2023. https://regionaldashboard.alberta.ca/region/cold-lake/population/#/?from=2018&to=2022

"Edmonton." 408 "Goose" Squadron. Accessed October and November 2023. http://www.forfreedom.ca/?page_id=111

Forsyth, Bruce. "The Mid-Canada Line." Canadian Military History by Bruce Forsyth. Accessed June 1, 2023. https://militarybruce.com/abandoned-canadian-military-bases/the-mid-canada-line/

"From the Journal's archives: A Prisoner Of War Counts Himself Lucky After Missing His Great Escape." The Edmonton Journal. June 14, 2016. https://edmontonjournal.com/news/local-news/from-the-journals-archives-a-prisoner-of-war-counts-himself-lucky-after-missing-his-great-escape

"Gulf War, 1990-1991." Veterans Affairs Canada. Last edited February 23, 2023. https://www.veterans.gc.ca/eng/remembrance/wars-and-conflicts/caf-operations/gulf-war

Bibliography

"Haiti, 1974-2010." Veterans Affairs Canada. Last edited December 7, 2023. https://www.veterans.gc.ca/eng/remembrance/wars-and-conflicts/caf-operations/haiti

March, William. "401 Squadron Provides Air Cover During Dieppe Raid." Government of Canada. August 19, 2019. https://www.canada.ca/en/department-national-defence/maple-leaf/rcaf/2019/09/401-squadron-provides-air-cover-during-dieppe-raid.html

"Memory Project: Stanley C. Gordon Gord King." The Canadian Encyclopedia. August 3, 2022. https://www.thecanadianencyclopedia.ca/en/article/mpsb-stanley-c-gordon-gord-king

Mulberry, Larry. *Aviation in Canada: The Pioneer Decades*. Toronto: Canav Books, 2008.

"Post-Second World War RCAF." RCAF Association. Specifically information on 401, 403, 409, 410, 417, 418, 419. https://www.rcafassociation.ca/heritage/history/post-second-world-war-rcaf/

"RCAF and the Crucible War." RCAF Association. Specifically information on 403, 408, 409, 410, 417, 418, 419 at the following: https://www.rcafassociation.ca/heritage/history/rcaf-and-the-crucible-of-war/403-squadron/ https://www.rcafassociation.ca/heritage/history/rcaf-and-the-crucible-of-war/408-squadron/ https://www.rcafassociation.ca/heritage/history/rcaf-and-the-crucible-of-war/409-squadron/ https://www.rcafassociation.ca/heritage/history/rcaf-and-the-crucible-of-war/410-squadron/ https://www.rcafassociation.ca/heritage/history/rcaf-and-the-crucible-of-war/410-squadron/ https://www.rcafassociation.ca/heritage/history/rcaf-and-the-crucible-of-war/418-squadron/ https://www.rcafassociation.ca/heritage/history/rcaf-and-the-crucible-of-war/419-squadron/

"RAF Bomber Command's first 1,000 bomber raid May 1942." Royal Air Force. Accessed September 2023. https://www.memorialflightclub.com/bomber-command-first-bomber-raid

"Taylor, Frederick Stuart." Second World War Service Records– War Dead, 1939-1947. Government of Canada. https://recherche-collection-search.bac-lac.gc.ca/eng/home/record?app=kia&IdNumber=34986&q=Fredrick%20Stuart%20Taylor

van der Drift, Nicky. "The Great Escape Tunnels." International Bomber Command Centre. April 28, 2021. https://internationalbcc.co.uk/about-ibcc/news/the-great-escape-tunnel/

Vaughan, Arnold P. *418: City of Edmonton Squadron History*. Belleville, Ontario: The Hanger Bookshelf, 1984.

"Wilfrid Reid May." Canada's Aviation Hall of Fame. Accessed January 2024. https://cahf.ca/wilfrid-reid-may/

Thank you for completing *The RCAF in Alberta: A Brief History*.

We would love if you could help by posting a review at your book retailer and on the PageMaster Publishing site. It only takes a minute and it would really help others by giving them an idea of your experience.

Thanks

https://pagemasterpublishing.ca/shop/The-RCAF-in-Alberta

To order more copies of this book, find books by other Canadian authors, or make inquiries about publishing your own book, contact PageMaster at:

PageMaster Publication Services Inc.
11340-120 Street, Edmonton, AB T5G 0W5
books@pagemaster.ca
780-425-9303

catalogue and e-commerce store
PageMasterPublishing.ca/Shop

Manufactured by Amazon.ca
Bolton, ON